CHRISTIAN HEROES: THEN & NOW

JOHN WESLEY

The World
His Parish

CHRISTIAN HEROES: THEN & NOW

JOHN WESLEY

The World His Parish

JANET & GEOFF BENGE

YWAM
PUBLISHING
P.O. BOX 55787   SEATTLE, WA 98155

YWAM Publishing is the publishing ministry of Youth With A Mission. Youth With A Mission (YWAM) is an international missionary organization of Christians from many denominations dedicated to presenting Jesus Christ to this generation. To this end, YWAM has focused its efforts in three main areas: (1) training and equipping believers for their part in fulfilling the Great Commission (Matthew 28:19), (2) personal evangelism,

For a free catalog of books and materials, call (425) 771-1153 or (800) 922-2143. Visit us online at www.ywampublishing.com.

John Wesley: The World His Parish
Copyright © 2007 by YWAM Publishing

Published by YWAM Publishing
a ministry of Youth With A Mission
P.O. Box 55787, Seattle, WA 98155

Second printing 2011

Library of Congress Cataloging-in-Publication Data
Benge, Janet, 1958–
  John Wesley : the world, his parish / Janet and Geoff Benge.
    p. cm. — (Christian heroes, then & now)
  Includes bibliographical references.
  ISBN 1-57658-382-1
  1. Wesley, John, 1703–1791—Juvenile literature. 2. Methodist Church—England—Clergy—Biography—Juvenile literature. I. Benge, Geoff, 1954– II. Title. III. Series.
  BX8495.W5B44 2007
  287.092—dc22
  [B]   2006100152

Unless otherwise noted, Scripture quotations in this book are taken from the King James Version of the Bible.

ISBN-13: 978-1-57658-382-1; ISBN-10: 1-57658-382-1

Printed in the United States of America

CHRISTIAN HEROES: THEN & NOW

*Unit study curriculum guides
are available for select biographies.*

*Available at your local Christian
bookstore or from YWAM Publishing
1-800-922-2143 / www.ywampublishing.com*

The narrative style of *John Wesley: The World His Parish* differs from that of other Christian Heroes: Then & Now biographies in regard to point of view. Normally the biographies are written from the subject's perspective, giving readers a focused slice of history from one person's viewpoint. *John Wesley* is written from a broader angle, encompassing the thoughts, opinions, and actions of not only Wesley but also other significant individuals.

The eighteenth century was a period of rapid change in Europe and America, and the evangelistic movement that Wesley was a part of was not localized, nor was it the work of only a few people. Together with his brother Charles and George Whitefield, Wesley founded Methodism, a movement that began in England and grew simultaneously in America. The wider narrative perspective in this book showcases the many important people and events which would have figured less prominently in a narrative limited to Wesley's perspective.

In all other aspects, we expect readers to enjoy the same familiar storytelling style in *John Wesley: The World His Parish* as they do in the rest of the Christian Heroes: Then & Now series.

—The Publisher

The British Isles

Contents

Chapter 1

Given Up for Dead

John Wesley was five years old when his life was totally altered by some sparks on a thatched roof. Until this time John's life—and the lives of his six sisters and two brothers—had been lived in a wholly religious atmosphere. John's father, Samuel Wesley, was the rector (another word for minister or priest) of a remote Anglican church in the English village of Epworth, located twenty miles from London. Epworth was part of the Fens district, which consisted of marshes and low-lying areas that regularly flooded. The area had very few roads.

The Wesley family had endured significant hardships. The Reverend Samuel Wesley, after relocating to the small Church of England parish in Epworth, faced hostile church members who didn't like his stern practices. As a result, he wound up in prison for a time. John's mother, Susanna Wesley, had given birth to many children, several of whom died at birth or in infancy. To make matters worse, Susanna struggled physically through each pregnancy, and this made life especially difficult.

Through all the hardship, Susanna continued to raise and teach her children, always trying to shield them from the realities of life around them. Her teaching efforts proved largely successful, because the Wesleys' eldest son, Samuel, had won a place at Westminster School in London in preparation for attending university at Oxford. When Samuel left Epworth for London, young John assumed that his life would follow the same path as his older brother's and that in several years he, too, would be heading to London to prepare for university.

On February 9, 1709, having settled into the family routine, John and his seven siblings still at home had gone to bed, anticipating another day of school and chores. John shared a bedroom in the attic with the family's nursemaid and several of the small children. In the middle of the night, John woke up from a sound sleep, opened his eyes, and noticed a glow around him. At first he thought the light came from an unusually bright sunrise, until he smelled smoke and heard a roaring sound. He tore back the curtain that surrounded his bed to see a room of empty beds and flames licking at the doorway. Alone in a burning house, he obviously could not escape through the door and down the stairs. He looked around quickly for another means of escape—the window!

Despite the desperate situation, John felt strangely calm as he dragged the dresser up to the window and climbed onto it. He could see his father, mother, and siblings half-clothed and shivering in the front yard two stories below. He glanced behind him to see the attic filling with smoke as the orange flames crept closer and closer to him along the floorboards. He knew that this was an image he would never forget—if he lived to remember it. What John didn't know was that the rest of his family had given him up for dead and were praying to commend his spirit to God.

Chapter 2

A Strict Regime

John's parents, Samuel Wesley and Susanna Annesley, first met at Samuel's sister's wedding in 1682 and were married in 1688, the same month that King William III and Queen Mary ascended to the English throne. Following Samuel and Susanna's wedding, John's father earned a living as the curate (an assistant clergyman) at St. Botolph Church in Aldersgate, London. He supplemented his income by writing religious booklets and poems, which his brother-in-law published for him. These works bore odd names like *The Grunting of a Hog*, *The Tame Snake in the Box of Bran*, and *A Hat Broke at Cugels*. After serving at St. Botolph Church, Samuel briefly took up church positions in Newington Butts, Surrey, and South Ormsby.

In 1695 the Marquess of Normanby, a high-ranking British nobleman, offered Samuel a lifelong position as rector of St. Andrews in Epworth. The position came with a decent salary of 130 pounds per year and the use of the church farmland called the glebe. In taking up the new position, Samuel promised himself that he would continue with his religious writings.

Part of the reason Samuel accepted the position as rector was his fast-growing family. In the seven years of Samuel and Susanna's marriage, Susanna, who was herself the youngest of twenty-five children, had given birth to six children, three of whom had survived the perils of infant diseases and were still alive when their parents made the move to Epworth. The oldest surviving child was a son, Samuel, followed by two daughters, Emilia and Susanna. Mrs. Wesley was pregnant with another child, who was born soon after the family arrived in Epworth. The Wesleys named this child, another daughter, Mary.

Although the position of rector at Epworth paid moderately well, Samuel Wesley lacked financial sense, and despite Susanna's best efforts, the family never had quite enough money to go around. The situation was made worse by the fact that Susanna gave birth to a new baby every year and was not well during her pregnancies. As was usual in such situations, the Wesleys employed a cook, a maid, and a nursemaid to take care of the children and the family's needs, adding significantly to their financial burden.

Life in Epworth was shockingly different for the Wesleys from what they had known in London. Both Samuel and Susanna had been raised by fathers who lived during a particularly turbulent period of English history. Samuel's father, also named Samuel Wesley, and Susanna's father, John Annesley, were both Dissenters, people who found fault with the ways of the Church of England and formed their own churches outside of the Church of England, the "Established Church." Both men were supporters of Oliver Cromwell, who overthrew King Charles I and set up a parliamentary commonwealth in which both Samuel and John served as ministers. However, when the monarchy was restored to power in 1660 and King Charles II took the throne, the two men were expelled from their church positions. Samuel and Susanna, however, did not follow in their fathers' dissenting ways but instead returned to the Church of England.

Susanna was particularly affected by the move to Epworth because she came from a lively, intellectual family that lived in the heart of London. At a time when only one in four women could sign her name, Susanna could read and write both English and French. She loved to debate various points of view about the Bible and theology (the study of the nature of God and religious beliefs), along with the views of her favorite philosopher, John Locke. But now Susanna found herself living permanently in one of the dullest and most unsophisticated regions of England. Nonetheless, she was determined to raise a cultured and God-fearing family, and she forbade her children from mixing with the local children for fear they would learn their coarse ways.

The local men and boys eked out their livings on the marshes, or fens, as they were called, that surrounded Epworth. On the fens they caught frogs, turtles, fish, and eels to eat and sell. Unfortunately the locals' lifestyle was under siege. The village of Epworth was located on the Isle of Axholme, a tiny island created by the weaving of five rivers, the Idle, Torr, Trent, Ouse, and Don, which crisscrossed the fens, making it difficult to travel any other way than on a sturdy horse, in a skiff, or on foot.

Eighty years earlier, the fens had been partly drained by a Dutch engineer in order to turn the rich layer of silt formed by the marshes into productive pastureland. The fensmen, however, did not want to be sheep or dairy farmers and had fought back every way they could. They were fighting a losing battle, though, as more and more land came under cultivation, and this led the locals to resent any outsiders who crossed their paths. That was exactly how the locals viewed the Wesleys when the family arrived in Epworth and took up residence in the old wood-and-plaster rectory, the house where the rector lived.

In truth, the people had shown little support for the Church of England clergyman whom Samuel Wesley had replaced, and they showed even less support for Samuel once he began preaching. Samuel was a fiery preacher, an expert at pointing out other people's wrongs, and a stickler for obeying church rules. He insisted that the "sinners" in his parish (church community) publicly confess their sins and outwardly express their regrets by standing barefoot for hours on the church's stone floor. The locals showed their displeasure at this message by destroying the Wesleys' flax crop growing in the glebe and by trying to kill the Wesleys' family dog, a mastiff.

Samuel and Susanna tried to insulate their children from this harsh, new reality. Susanna governed the children with military precision. She began teaching each child to recite the Lord's Prayer morning and night as soon as the child could talk and to memorize large sections—sometimes entire books—of the Bible. Then on each child's fifth birthday, the child would learn the alphabet and begin reading the following day. Since the Bible was the children's only textbook, the first word each Wesley child learned to read was "in," followed by "the beginning God created the heaven and the earth." The children's school week lasted six days, Monday through Saturday, from nine in the morning till five in the evening, with a two-hour break for lunch. Sunday was the only day off. By the time he was twelve, Samuel, the oldest child, was already excelling in Latin and Greek.

It was into this strict upbringing that John Benjamin Wesley was born on June 17, 1703. In the eight years since the Wesleys had moved into the rectory at Epworth, Susanna had given birth to numerous children following Mary's birth, but only two had survived birth and infancy—Mehetabel, who was called Hetty, and Anne. When he was born, John, Susanna's fifteenth child, had one older brother and five older sisters. He was named after his grandfather Dr. John Annesley and his uncle Benjamin Annesley, and his parents hoped that he would fare better than his two deceased older brothers who had both borne the name John Benjamin before him. John's birth was duly noted in the family Bible, and life went on in the rectory.

During this time, John's father was deeply in debt and more unpopular than ever in Epworth. The year before, he had taken a disastrous stand against the popular Dissenter candidate in local elections. In retaliation, one of his parishioners (church members) had demanded payment for a loan he had made to Samuel. Since Samuel lacked the money to repay the debt, he was locked up in Lincoln Debtors' Prison. Susanna soldiered on while her husband was imprisoned, making ends meet and waiting for the archbishop to come to the family's aid. The archbishop did so, and after three months in prison, Samuel was released to return to his parish.

Following John's birth, more children were added to the financially strapped family. Another son was born in 1706, but he was accidentally smothered to death while sleeping with his nursemaid. Two more babies followed in quick succession—Martha, who was not quite three years younger than John, and Charles, who was four and a half years younger. When John's brother Samuel left to study at

Westminster School in London, the crowded Wesley household was happy and somewhat relieved.

Everything changed on a cold, winter night in 1709 when a burning timber fell across the foot of twelve-year-old Hetty's bed. Jolted awake, Hetty looked up to see the roof on fire. She jumped out of bed and ran into her father's bedroom and woke him, and her father in turn roused the rest of the family. Everyone scrambled out of bed and raced down the stairs together. The family had to wait at the bottom of the staircase because the Reverend Wesley had left the key to the locked front door upstairs beside his bed. Wincing from the smoke in his eyes, he rushed back up the burning staircase, grabbed the key, and sprinted out of the room. The staircase, now on fire, collapsed behind him as he charged down it. He quickly unlocked the front door, and the family spilled out into the yard.

The only person who did not rush out the door was John, who was still sound asleep in the attic bedroom, unaware that anything was wrong. Although John shared this room with others, he had a curtain around his bed, and no one had noticed that he was still sleeping as the nursemaid and the other children rushed from the room screaming. It was not until everyone had left the house that John finally awoke. By this time the rest of the family had lost hope for him, and they knelt down to pray to commit him to the Lord.

Thankfully for John, not everyone at the scene had the same idea. One of the neighbors who had come to watch the spectacle spotted John at the window and yelled out. The Wesleys looked up and saw John, and everyone set frantically to work to save him. Since no ladders were available nearby, several men stood on each other's shoulders until they were able to get high enough to reach John's window. The man at the top of the stacked-up men stretched out, pulled the shutters aside, and grabbed John by the neck, wrenching the boy out the window. Moments later John found himself on the ground, now safely part of the scene he had been watching from above.

John's mother hugged her son tightly, and his father shook his head in amazement. "This boy is a brand plucked from the burning fire!" he exclaimed. "Let us give thanks to God! He has given me my eight children. Let the house go. I am rich enough."

As the Wesley family watched their home burn, the Reverend Wesley concluded that someone had deliberately set the house on fire. The fire had started in the dead of night and in the thatched roof, which was not the normal way a house fire started. Samuel decided that some disgruntled parishioner had started it.

The fire smoldered until dawn, and by then everything in the house had been destroyed, including Samuel Wesley's manuscript for his commentary on the book of Job, which was ready for the printer, his library of Greek and Latin books, and a set of valuable papers by Dr. John Annesley, along with all of the family's clothes and food and the money from the last flax harvest.

Relief at surviving the fire soon gave way to the reality of the new situation. The Wesley family—a minister, his eight-months-pregnant wife, and eight children ranging in age from a little over a year to seventeen years old—were homeless and penniless. The situation was dire, and Samuel Wesley could see no way that his family could all stay together, at least for the foreseeable future. He and Susanna set about dividing their children among family members, friends, and parishioners who were willing to take them in. Two girls, Susanna and Hetty, were sent to London to stay with their uncle Matthew Wesley, while John and others were farmed out to local families. Emilia, the oldest daughter, was needed to help prepare for the arrival of the new baby, so Samuel and Susanna, Emilia, and little Charles boarded in a nearby house.

Within twenty-four hours of the fire, the Wesley family had scattered, and John was left alone with a family that just a day before his mother would have forbidden him to even talk to. He could hardly believe the lax life this family lived.

Chapter 3

Reforming the Family

At first John was shocked at what the sons of his adoptive family were allowed to do. It was unbelievable to him. The boys ran in and out of the house as they pleased, wrestled in the yard, ate snacks between meals, and called each other by their first names without using the term *brother* first. But as time went by, John grew used to his new life. He hunted for frogs and eels on the fens and visited his new friends in their homes at any time of the day or night.

The only time John's family, minus Susanna and Hetty who were in London, were together was at church on Sunday mornings. During the service the Wesley children had to sit in the front pew under the stern glare of their father. Their mother attended the services too, though she left the latest addition to the family, baby Kezziah, at home with Emilia. Kezziah was named after one of the daughters of Job, a man in the Old Testament who underwent all sorts of terrible trials. No doubt Samuel and Susanna Wesley felt that the name suited the situation they found themselves in.

A new rectory was being constructed using bricks so that it would not burn down quite so easily. Each day John watched the progress on the family's replacement home. He found it difficult to imagine his entire family living happily together again under its roof. The life the family had lived in the old rectory seemed so far away to him now.

Finally, one year after the fire, work on the new rectory was finished, and the Wesley family were reunited. Samuel and Susanna, new baby Kezziah, and two-year-old Charles moved in first. Samuel and Susanna then collected their other children from the families they had been staying with on the fens, and finally Susanna and Hetty returned from London, full of ideas about becoming governesses.

Susanna Wesley was appalled when she realized the extent of the influence that others had had on her children. The children ran around at will, yelled in the house, recited rude ditties, and spoke with the thick accent of those who lived on the fens, an accent their mother described as "clownish." Reformation of her children's character was needed, and Susanna was just the person to do it. In her methodical way she made up a list of rules by which her children's behavior would be measured. Violators of the new rules would be punished as a warning to the rest of the children that they must fall into line.

The rules included rewards for positive behavior as well as punishment for negative actions. If one of the children was guilty of a character fault and confessed it before he or she was caught, the child would not be punished. And as long as a child was trying his or her hardest to do the right thing, he or she would be encouraged and guided to do so. However, if any of the children were caught in a sinful act, such as lying, dishonoring the Lord's Day, being disobedient, or quarrelling, they would receive the rod as punishment. In addition, if anyone made a promise to give away something to another person, the item became that person's property permanently; the one who had given it had no right to ask for it back under any circumstances. Another rule was that no girl should be made to do household chores until she could read well.

Other changes were implemented in the family as well. The children learned to sing psalms and chanted them four times a day, and they were permanently paired up, the oldest with the youngest, the second oldest with the second youngest, and so on. John and Hetty became a pair, and Hetty read John a chapter from the New Testament and a psalm before school started each day and a chapter from the Old Testament and another psalm at the end of class.

Soon Susanna decided that more steps were needed to bring her wayward children back into line. She started taking one child aside for an hour each night of the week to quiz the child on his or her spiritual progress and answer any questions he or she might have about the Bible or theology. John's evening for this individual attention was Thursday, and John asked more questions than any of the other children. His mother noted his logical way of looking at things and answered her seven-year-old's concerns with dignity and respect.

Eventually the rules and Susanna's force of will helped restore a sense of unity to the family, but the children were never as insulated from the life of the community around them as they had been before the fire. As a result of their having been scattered among so many different families, all of the children had been exposed to other ways of life, and at times they fought against the life they were being forced to resume. Years later, in a letter to John, Susanna Wesley wrote about the effects of the fire upon her family.

> For some years we went on very well. Never were children in better order. Never were children better disposed to piety, or in more subjection to their parents, till that fatal dispersion of them, after the fire, into several families.

Two years after the reunification of the family, Samuel Wesley set out for an extended visit to London. He had been chosen to represent his church district at a convocation (a large, formal assembly) of Anglican leaders. What Samuel could not have known as he set out was that while he was gone, his wife would hold a convocation of her own at Epworth—a situation that would severely test his ideas about the role of women in church leadership.

At the time of the Reverend Wesley's departure for London at New Year 1712, about twenty-five parishioners could be nudged or persuaded to attend church on any given Sunday. Later, however, when Samuel returned, two to three hundred people, all of them as a direct result of Susanna's efforts, willingly attended service.

The whole affair began when Emilia noticed a book that had been donated to her father to help restock his library after the fire. This book told the story of two Danish men, Ziegenbalg and Pluteshau, who had responded to an urgent request from the king of Denmark for missionaries. In September 1706 these two men had arrived in Tranquebar on the southeast coast of India, becoming the first Protestant (non–Roman Catholic) missionaries to that country. The pair began preaching the gospel and baptized their first converts about ten months after arriving in Tranquebar. But Hindus and the local Danish authorities both opposed their work, and in 1707–08 Ziegenbalg spent four months in prison on a charge that by converting the locals to Christianity, he was encouraging rebellion.

Emilia was so intrigued with the story of the two men and the selections of their powerful sermons contained in the book that she began reading aloud from it to her mother. Soon the whole family wanted to listen, and Susanna took to reading passages aloud from the book following the children's afternoon prayer and Bible-reading time.

The dramatic story of the two missionaries even attracted the attention of the servants in the house, and within two weeks of Samuel Wesley's departure for London, the servants had spread word of the story around Epworth and across the fens. Soon neighbors began inquiring as to when and whether Mrs. Wesley might hold public readings from the book.

Ordinarily Susanna might have shied away from such a suggestion, but she was spurred on by the behavior of the Reverend Inman, the minister that the archbishop had sent to Epworth as a substitute in Samuel Wesley's absence. Like so many others before him, Mr. Inman used the pulpit as a means to communicate his pet peeves, chief among which was the unrighteousness of being in debt. Week after week he would bombard the Wesley family and other occasional visitors to the church with threats of God's wrath on all who did not pay their bills. Apart from the fact that it was very boring to hear the same sermon over and over, the topic enraged Susanna Wesley. Everyone in the village knew that her husband had been locked up in debtors' prison for a time and that he still struggled to be financially responsible, especially since the family had lost everything in the fire. She felt sure that Mr. Inman intended to rub salt in the wound.

Susanna contrasted the Reverend Inman's repetitive, droning sermons against the lively accounts of

the two Danish missionaries recorded in the book
and decided in favor of the missionaries. She opened
the rectory on Sunday afternoons to a public meeting, which was held in the kitchen. Within a month
two hundred people were attending the meetings.
As many people as possible crammed into the
kitchen, and the overflow spread into the hallway
while others stood outside and listened through the
open window.

Of course, Mr. Inman took these unauthorized
meetings seriously, especially since they were much
more popular than his own church meetings. He
wrote a letter of complaint to Samuel Wesley in
London, pointing out the obvious. Susanna could be
getting herself into legal trouble because her meetings were not registered with the state as a Dissenter
meeting, nor were they officially approved by the
Church of England. In short, Susanna Wesley, the
wife of an Anglican minister, was holding illegal
meetings.

Samuel wrote a strong letter to his wife in which
he pointed out that it was not normal to hold such
meetings, especially in a church rectory and guided
by a woman. He suggested that Susanna ask a man
to read the book aloud. His suggestion did not sit
well with Susanna, and as her husband's intellectual
and spiritual equal, she refused to back down. In
response she wrote,

> As to it looking particular [peculiar], I grant
> it does. And so does everything that is seri-
> ous or that may [in] any way advance the

glory of God or the salvation of souls if it be performed out of a pulpit, or in the way of common conversation, because in our corrupt age, the utmost care and diligence have to be used to banish all discourse of God or spiritual concerns out of our society....

As I am a woman, so I am also the mistress of a large family. And though the superior charge of the souls contained in it lies upon you, as head of the family, and as their minister; yet in your absence I cannot but look upon every soul you leave under my care as a talent committed to me.

The mail was delivered once a week to Epworth, and Susanna used the opportunity to debate with her husband by letter. Samuel suggested that the meetings stop, while Susanna argued that the meetings were doing so much good in the community.

Our meeting has wonderfully conciliated the minds of this people toward us, so that we now live in the greatest amity imaginable.... Some families who seldom went to church, now go constantly; and one person, who had not been there for seven years, is now prevailed upon to go with the rest.

She finished her letter with these words:

If you do, after all, think fit to dissolve this assembly, do not tell me any more that you desire me to do it, for that will not satisfy my conscience; but send me your positive command, in such full and express terms as may absolve me from all guilt and punishment, for neglecting this opportunity of doing good to souls, when you and I shall appear before the great and awful tribunal of our Lord Jesus Christ.

Samuel did not forbid his wife to continue, though the meetings were curtailed when smallpox struck the village of Epworth. John and four of his sisters were stricken with the disease, but under Susanna's regimented care, they all made full recoveries.

When Samuel returned from London, the meetings were disbanded in favor of church services, but the benefits remained. Church attendance continued to rise, and the Wesleys lived at peace with their neighbors. John, who was one of his mother's staunchest supporters, took note of the positive effects of the "society" that had blossomed in the rectory kitchen, and there is no doubt that the experience played a part in directing his future.

In 1714, the time came for eleven-year-old John Wesley to follow in his brother Samuel's footsteps and go away to school. On one of his trips to London, the Reverend Wesley had arranged for the Duke of Buckingham to sponsor John at the Charterhouse School in the capital city.

John's sisters, though, had not been sent off to school, because there were very few private boarding schools for girls. This meant that the two oldest girls, Emilia and Susanna, who were now twenty-two and nineteen, respectively, had no prospects other than marriage or being governesses. At the same time that eleven-year-old John was being out-fitted with a black broadcloth robe, knee pants, and new boots, Susanna Wesley was doing all she could to find a way to furnish her two oldest daughters with enough suitable clothes to leave the rectory in search of governess positions. John was oblivious to the envy his sisters felt at the opportunities awaiting him. He had never before traveled more than five miles away from Epworth, and the idea of going alone to London both fascinated and terrified him.

Chapter 4

A Diligent Student

John arrived at the Charterhouse School in London with little idea of what lay ahead. He soon discovered that an established pecking order existed among the students, with the smallest of the new students being on the very bottom rung. This meant that John had to spend many hours running errands for the older boys, cleaning their shoes, and allowing them to take food off his plate in the dining room. John soon realized that this was the way things were done at English boarding schools, and he knew that if he endured, he would move up the pecking order the next year and be able to require the same of a new batch of freshmen.

At first John struggled with homesickness, longing for the strict life he had left behind in Epworth.

His entire life had been spent under the direct spiritual guidance of his mother and, to a lesser extent, his father, and now he missed that guidance. For the first time since the fire that burned down the rectory, John was free to think what he liked and do things without anyone inquiring about his motives. As a result he soon felt himself slipping from the high ideals he had set for himself. John decided to write a list of things he felt he had to do to be in right standing with God. These were (1) "not being so bad as other people," (2) "having still a kindness for religion," and (3) "reading the Bible, going to church, and saying my prayers." These rules, which John did his best to keep, may have seemed very pious to most of his fellow students, but for a Wesley they represented the bare minimum of acceptable behavior.

John enjoyed his first year at Charterhouse School. The lessons were not particularly challenging to him, despite the fact that he had to speak Latin all day and learn Greek and Hebrew. Since it was too expensive for him to return to Epworth on a regular basis, John often spent holidays and weekends with his brother Samuel and his new wife, Ursula, or with his Wesley and Annesley relatives in London.

In 1715 John's younger brother Charles joined John in London. He attended Westminster School, where their father had arranged a scholarship for him. On special occasions all three Wesley brothers got together, something John always looked forward to.

Meanwhile, back in Epworth the residents of the rectory experienced mysterious events just before

Christmas 1716. The parlor maid swore that she heard strange knocking sounds coming from inside the rectory walls. The woman became so frightened by the sounds that Susanna consulted a neighbor as to what the noise might be.

"Ah, it must be rats," the neighbor told her. "I had rats in the walls of my house that made a sound like that. But I fixed the trouble. I blew my trumpet in the house as loud as I could, and they all scurried away, never to return."

Susanna borrowed the neighbor's trumpet and blew the instrument as loud as she could throughout the house. Satisfied she had rid the rectory of rats, she returned the trumpet. Despite her effort, however, the parlor maid continued to complain of hearing noises in the walls.

Then Emilia reported hearing unexplained groaning sounds in the rectory, followed by the sound of breaking glass in the kitchen. Terrified, she ran to her mother, who went to investigate. In the kitchen Susanna found nothing broken or out of place. But that was not the end of it. Soon afterward the butler insisted that in the middle of the night he heard dragging sounds on the stairs and a loud tapping noise coming from inside the walls and the ceilings and under the floorboards. There seemed to be no logical explanation for the noises people in the house were hearing, and everyone reached the conclusion that the rectory was haunted. Even Susanna Wesley was finally won over to this conclusion, and they all took to calling the ghost Old Jeffrey, after a man in the village who had taken his own life.

While everyone else in the rectory believed that the place was haunted, Samuel Wesley refused to accept such a conclusion. He argued that there had to be some logical explanation that they had not yet found. But even Samuel changed his mind when he too began hearing strange noises emanating from the rectory walls.

John heard of the strange happenings at the rectory in a letter he received from his sister Anne. At first he was amused by what he read, but as letters continued to arrive from Epworth giving more details of the strange haunting, he grew more fascinated with what was happening. He wrote home pressing for more details. His mother wrote in response, "I cannot imagine how you should be so curious about our unwelcome guest. For my part, I am quite tired with hearing or speaking about it: but if you come among us, you will find enough to satisfy all your scruples, and perhaps may hear or see it yourself."

When the Wesley brothers next got together, they spent many hours discussing the haunting of the rectory at Epworth they had been reading about in their letters from home. At first John found it hard to accept that his family had taken to believing in ghosts, especially since he knew that his mother and father would normally have called such a belief the invention of an idle and undisciplined mind. But since their parents both believed that the haunting was real, the three brothers concluded that indeed it must be true.

Three months after the first mention of Old Jeffrey, news came that the strange events had stopped and the rectory had returned to normal. This information came as a relief to John. Now he could once again concentrate fully on his studies, but he never forgot the incident that led him to believe that supernatural powers were at work in the world.

Nothing as remotely interesting as a haunted rectory happened during the remainder of John's time attending Charterhouse School. At the end of his term at the school, John had done so well with his studies that the Charterhouse School offered him a scholarship of twenty pounds toward his college education. John applied to Christ Church at Oxford. The college accepted his application and matched the amount of the scholarship from the Charterhouse School, allowing him to continue his studies.

On June 14, 1720, John entered Christ Church, the most prestigious college at Oxford, following in the footsteps of his older brother. Three days later he turned seventeen. John found the course work in logic, rhetoric, politics, and morals interesting and easy to pass. He was also in full charge of his leisure activities and was soon filling his days with boating, chess, card games, dancing, theater, tennis, and billiards. As he pursued these activities, his ideas of faith and serving God slipped further away from his everyday experience. The simple standards he had established for himself at the Charterhouse School seemed harder than ever to keep in light of these new pursuits. John rarely thought about his spiritual condition apart from the twice-yearly Communion service where he was obliged to examine his sinful state.

John watched over his money as closely as he could, but sometimes he found himself in the embarrassing situation of needing to ask his friends or tutors for loans. Like his father before him, John saw his debts beginning to grow.

Meanwhile, things were not going well back at the rectory at Epworth, specifically for John's older sisters. They were all well educated and spoke Latin and Greek, but the family lived in one of the most backward areas of England. And because their father was such a poor financial manager, the Wesley sisters did not have enough fine clothes or life experiences to present themselves as eligible brides in the level of society for which they had been groomed. Emilia was able to find a job working as a teacher in a boarding school in Lincoln, but the next sister, Susanna, chose a more difficult solution. While staying with her uncle in London, she met and then married a farmer named Richard Ellison without her parents' permission. When Samuel and Susanna Wesley met Richard Ellison, they were appalled at his coarse behavior, and they were horrified when they learned that he was an abusive husband. John's mother described him as "a little inferior to the apostate angels of wickedness." News of his sister's marriage to such a man as Richard Ellison saddened John as he continued his studies at Oxford.

One day in the summer of 1723, John took a walk alone in the country. When he stopped to rest beside a stream, he noticed that his nose had begun to bleed. At first he was not too concerned, but as the minutes ticked by and he could not get the bleeding to stop, John began to worry that he might bleed to death. Finally, in desperation he jumped into the cold water of the stream. The sudden shock seemed to stem the flow of blood, and a soggy and shivering John set off for home. As he trudged along, he promised himself that he would pay closer attention to his health and well-being.

In the library at Oxford, John began to search for the latest information available on living a healthy life. One book caught his attention. The book was titled *Dr. Cheyne's Book of Health and Long Life*, and John read it from cover to cover. Unlike many theories of the day that promoted bloodletting and the use of purgatives as cures for sickness, Dr. Cheyne's approach was more preventative. Dr. Cheyne urged his readers to take control of their own health by consuming moderate amounts of food and drink and by exercising regularly. John made a list of foods that Dr. Cheyne considered unhealthy, including anything salted or highly seasoned, as well as pork, fish, and stall-fed cattle. The doctor recommended drinking two pints of water a day, along with eating a total of eight ounces of meat and twelve ounces of vegetables. As far as exercise was concerned, Dr. Cheyne recommended lots of it. He was particularly impressed with horse riding, which "promoted a universal perspiration," and stated that everyone should be in bed by eight o'clock at night and arise at four in the morning. John did his best to follow the advice in the book, and soon he began to notice an improvement in his health.

Shortly after his twenty-first birthday on June 17, 1724, John received a pleasant surprise. His brother Samuel wrote to say that their mother was coming to London to greet her brother who was returning from India. John was surprised that his mother had decided to make the arduous journey, as she had not been to London since long before he was born. Still, he was delighted to think that the event could mark a turnaround in the Wesley family's fortunes. Uncle Samuel Annesley was a prominent trader with the East India Company who had made a fortune in India. He had written to Susanna promising that upon his return to England he would give his sister the enormous sum of one thousand pounds in order to get the Wesleys out of debt and set them on a better financial footing. John's mother then wrote to say that she would use some of the money to pay off John's debts as well, possibly allowing John to continue at Christ Church to earn a master's degree.

John traveled to London from Oxford and he, Samuel, and Charles met their mother when she arrived by stagecoach from Epworth. They accompanied her to the dock to await the arrival of the ship carrying her brother. Finally the vessel sailed up the Thames River and tied up alongside the dock, but Samuel Annesley was not aboard. The vessel's captain did not know why he had not sailed with them when they left India, and no one aboard could give them any information about what had happened to him. There was nothing to do but write to India and wait for a reply from Samuel. But the reply never came. Samuel Annesley and his fortune had disappeared forever. The family suspected foul play, but they were too far away to pursue any investigation. John learned a bitter lesson in counting on money that was promised to him.

When she arrived back in Epworth, Susanna wrote to John. "Do not be discouraged; do your duty, keep close to your studies, and hope for better days."

Since his debts remained unpaid, John needed to cut back on his spending. He decided to grow his hair long to avoid the cost of buying a new wig. No one else he knew had his own head of long hair, though oddly enough the fashion of the day was for men to wear long-haired wigs. The fact that he grew out his hair did not bother John. In fact he joked about it in a letter to his mother. First he described how dangerous it was to be out at night in Oxford. One of his fellow students had been standing at the entrance to a coffeehouse at about seven o'clock in the evening when someone ran past and snatched both the student's cap and his wig from his head. John added, "I am pretty safe from such gentlemen, for unless they carried me away, carcass and all, they would have but a poor purchase."

John continued with his studies, unsure what he would do when he graduated from Christ Church. Because he had no family money behind him, his choices were limited to being either a teacher or a clergyman. Although he came from a line of distinguished ministers, John was not sure that he wanted to follow in their footsteps, yet he felt some pressure to do so. In 1724 John's father was given a second parish to watch over. The new parish was located in Wroot, about five miles from Epworth, but in winter the two villages were cut off from each other by the rising water of the marshlands. His responsibilities with the new parish paid Samuel Wesley an extra fifty pounds a year, though much of that money was spent employing an assistant curate to preach at one or the other of the churches. It seemed an obvious choice for John to return to Epworth and become his father's curate once he graduated. But the thought of preaching did not appeal to John, though he was not sure why. Then a chance meeting shed some light on the subject for him.

One chilly night as he entered the main door of the college, John struck up a conversation with the college porter. The porter had on only a light coat as he stood shivering by the door. John encouraged him to go and put on a warmer coat and drink some hot tea, but the porter responded that he was wearing the only coat he owned and all he had to drink each day was water. And even though he was shivering, he added that he thanked God for the coat he did have and the water he had to drink, as well as for the dry stones he would sleep upon that night.

John was surprised by the porter's reply, and he said, "You thank God when you have nothing to wear, nothing to eat, and no bed to lie upon. What else do you thank Him for?"

The porter looked John directly in the eye and said, "I thank Him that He has given me my life and being, and a heart to love Him, and a desire to serve Him."

As John lay in his bed that night, he thought about what the porter had said, and he asked himself some questions: Why didn't he feel that same love for God? How was the porter able to carry on with such a grateful attitude even though he had few material comforts? Could the porter have found the secret of a righteous life, while it had eluded him, a soon-to-be graduate of Christ Church? John did not know the answers to these troubling questions, but he knew that he would not stop searching until he found them.

The Quest for Meaning

Stirred by the questions the short conversation with the college porter had raised within him, John set out on a quest to find true spiritual meaning. It would prove to be a long and difficult journey. John started his quest by reading the book *The Rules of Holy Living and Dying* by Jeremy Taylor. But the book seemed to raise more questions than it answered. One of the questions it raised had to do with the notion of predestination. The Church of England taught that God predestines, or chooses in advance, the people who will become Christians and receive eternal life. This view was developed by the French theologian John Calvin and his Calvinist followers. According to this way of thinking, John realized that if he had become a Christian, it was not because he had freely chosen to do so but because he was following a set course that God had already planned for him. The opposing doctrine stated that each person freely makes his or her own decision to become a Christian and that even God does not know whether a person will make that choice. A Dutch theologian named Jacobus Arminius was the first to put forward this doctrine, which thus became known as Arminianism.

The more John thought about the issue, the more confused he became. He could see Bible verses that supported both views. Finally, as he often did when he was confused, John turned to his mother for advice. She, too, had struggled with the same question in her youth and was happy to share her conclusions with her son in a complex letter.

Dear Son,

I have often wondered that men should be so vain to amuse themselves by searching into the decrees of God, which no human wit can fathom; and do not rather employ their time and powers in working out their salvation, and making their own calling and election sure.

Such studies tend more to confound them than to inform the understanding; and young people have best let them alone. But...I will tell you my thoughts on the matter, and if they satisfy not, you may desire your father's direction, who is surely better qualified than me.

The doctrine of predestination as maintained by rigid Calvinists is very shocking, and ought to be abhorred because it charges the most holy God with being the author of sin. And I think you reason very well and justly against it; for it is certainly inconsistent with the justice and goodness of God....

[Yet] I do firmly believe that God, from all eternity, has elected some to everlasting life; but then I humbly conceive that this election is founded on his foreknowledge....

This is the sum of what I believe concerning predestination...; since it does in no wise detract from the glory of God's free grace, nor impair the liberty of man. Nor can it with more reason be supposed that the [foreknowledge] of God is the cause that so many finally perish, than our knowing the sun will rise tomorrow is the cause of the rising.

The letter settled the issue for John. He believed as his mother did, that God chose certain key people to become Christians and that the rest were left with free choice as to whether or not they would be saved and go to heaven.

But while John had settled the matter of predestination to his satisfaction, other issues soon arose to take its place. John talked with Lutherans and Calvinists alike about the role of faith and works in the Christian life. Was it enough to believe in Christ, he wondered, or did a Christian have to do good works to prove that he or she was saved? The opinions he received from others sent John around and around on this issue until eventually he had to accept the fact that he had no firm answer to this question.

All of this thinking about the Christian faith convinced John of one thing: his future lay in the church. When he graduated from Christ Church with his bachelor's degree in 1724, regardless of his tight financial situation, John immediately signed up to begin work on a master's degree while seeking to be ordained as a minister in the Church of England.

The following year turned out to be one of the most confusing years of all for John as he studied for his master's degree. This time his problem was not with theological issues but with young women— four young women to be exact. John's friend Robin Griffith introduced him to a new circle of friends in the Cotswold village of Stanton, west of Oxford. Whenever he had spare time, John walked or rode to Stanton to spend time picnicking, dancing, or discussing the latest literature with people. Even though he was short and not particularly handsome, on these visits John attracted the attention of many young women. He was serious about his faith, he was intelligent, and, most unusual of all for the time, he accepted women as his intellectual equals, since he had been raised by a well-educated mother and had been surrounded by seven witty and well-read sisters. These qualities soon made John the center of attention of four young women in particular who clung to every word he said. The young women were three sisters, Sally, Elizabeth, and Damaris Kirkman, and a twenty-year-old widow named Mary Pendarves. All four of these women were interested in marriage and saw John as a good possibility for a husband.

While the attention flattered John, he soon found himself confused by it, especially when he tried to talk to the women about loving God and about loving them. The situation grew complicated very fast, and before John knew it, he found himself unofficially engaged to be married to Sally Kirkman. Or at least he thought he was, but he could not be sure, because he was unable to bring himself to openly discuss his feelings for her. As a result, the relationship soon soured, and Sally eventually shunned John and married a local schoolteacher.

John was shocked and bewildered by the situation. He had come to rely heavily on Sally's insights and missed not being able to discuss all manner of things with her as he had once done. Eventually John somehow managed to salvage his friendship with Sally and the other three women. Before long he was writing to each of them, seeking their advice on matters and offering them advice when they asked for it. In one letter, Sally suggested that John read a book called *The Imitation of Christ* by the medieval German monk Thomas à Kempis. John took her advice and got a copy of the book from the library. The book challenged John's thinking and led him to the understanding that being a Christian meant having a complete change of heart and that there was no such thing as a half-hearted Christian—a person was either moving toward God or moving away from Him. As a result, John determined to do whatever was necessary to become a "whole" Christian with a heart completely changed by the love of God. With this goal in mind he wrote out a new set of guidelines to live by:

A General Rule in All Actions of Life
Whenever you are to do any action, consider how God did or would do the like, and... imitate His example.

General Rules for Employing Time
1. Begin and end every day with God; sleep not immoderately.
2. Be diligent in your calling.
3. Employ all spare hours in religion, as able.
4. Make all holidays holy days.
5. Avoid drunkards and busybodies.
6. Avoid curiosity, and all useless employments and knowledge.
7. Examine yourself every night.
8. Never on any account pass a day without setting aside at least an hour for devotion.
9. Avoid all manner of passion.

General Rules as to Intention
1. In every act reflect on the end.
2. Begin every action in the name of the Father, the Son and the Holy Ghost.
3. Begin every important work with prayer.

4. Do not leave off a duty because you are tempted to do it.

Twice a day and every Saturday night John took time to read through his list and make notes on how well he was doing in living up to his rules.

On October 19, 1725, at twenty-two years of age, John was ordained as a minister in the Church of England. He had a bright future ahead of him, though at that time the question weighing on his mind was whether to become a curate in some Anglican parish or apply to become a fellow at Lincoln College. Located in Oxford, Lincoln College was dedicated to giving young men from Lincolnshire an education. Accordingly, several teaching positions at the college could be filled only by teachers from Lincolnshire. And since Epworth was located in Lincolnshire, John had a good chance of being awarded a teaching position, even though he was still working on his master's degree.

Eventually John decided in favor of applying for a position at Lincoln College. He spent the following summer visiting influential churchmen in and around Lincolnshire whose favor could help him win the position he sought. Then he headed home to Epworth to visit his family. All was not well when he arrived there.

Earlier in the year, John's twenty-eight-year-old sister Hetty had fallen in love with a local lawyer. Samuel Wesley did not approve of the match and banned his daughter from seeing the man, but Hetty refused to accept her father's decision. The ugly situation grew worse when the lawyer, whom Hetty expected to marry, suddenly ran off, leaving her in disgrace. Samuel Wesley, now furious, ordered his daughter to marry the first man who asked for her hand. Unfortunately for Hetty, that man was a traveling plumber named William Wright, who happened to come to the rectory. Much to his amazement, the man walked away from the place with a new bride. As Hetty left, Samuel forbade her from ever returning to the rectory, telling her he would rather she had died than put the family through such an ordeal.

Susanna Wesley was heartbroken by what had happened. The other Wesley sisters were outraged by the harsh treatment of Hetty and stood up to the heavy-handed ways of their father. As a result, it was not a happy or harmonious home that John returned to.

To make matters worse, Samuel Wesley's health was deteriorating, and while John was home his father suffered a stroke that rendered his right hand useless. Doggedly, though, Samuel set about learning to write with his left hand.

At the end of summer John returned to Oxford, accompanied by his brother Charles, who had also enrolled at Christ Church. Back in Oxford John continued to study for his master's degree while he waited to see whether he would be appointed to a position at Lincoln College. The election to choose a new fellow for the college was postponed twice, and it was March before John learned that the position was his. By then the winter term was ending, and it was time for summer recess. John decided to return to Epworth and give his parents the good news. He had little money at the time and could not afford to take the stagecoach home, so he decided to walk the seventy-five miles. This took some time, but John was in fine physical shape when he finally arrived.

Back home in Epworth, John performed duties as the curate in the parish of Wroot, and he also helped his father finish the huge commentary he was writing on the book of Job to replace the manuscript burned in the rectory fire years before. During this time John took interest in a pretty, young woman. Sizing up the situation, Samuel banned the young woman from visiting the rectory in an attempt to keep his son's mind on his spiritual work. In addition, Samuel was still adamant that he would never again speak to his daughter Hetty, even though she was stuck in a miserable marriage and had lost a baby.

His father's attitude infuriated John so much that he preached a sermon on loving others, finishing it with the story of his sister and how his father was not living up to Christian standards in the way he was treating her. Of course Samuel was furious with his son for doing so, and John dutifully apologized, only to deliver a more scathing sermon the following Sunday. After this second sermon, months passed before father and son could again speak civilly to each other.

Relationships at the rectory were so tense that everyone breathed a sigh of relief when John returned to Oxford to begin his new position at Lincoln College. In theory John was responsible both for the spiritual welfare of a group of students and for teaching the students Greek, Latin, and philosophy. In reality, the college did not stress spiritual values, and John's classes met irregularly. This gave John plenty of time to finish his master's degree and take long trips to visit his family or other parishes.

The easy life came to a halt, however, in October 1729 when, on one of his trips away, John received a letter instructing him to return to Lincoln College and take a more active role in overseeing the spiritual well-being of the students or else resign his post as fellow.

The reason for the college's renewed interest in the spiritual welfare of the students was partly related to an upsurge in two fashionable but troublesome teachings. One, known as Arianism, denied that Christ was God, and the other, known as deism, stated that God does not communicate with mankind or intervene in mankind's affairs. The governors of Lincoln College were concerned that these two heresies were gaining followers in their midst, and they needed the college's fellows to intervene. Little did they know that John Wesley's required return to the college would not only change the moral climate there but also set off a series of events that would change the entire nation.

Chapter 6

A New Challenge

In response to the letter he received, John returned to Oxford, where he discovered that his younger brother Charles had started the "Holy Club" at Christ Church. The club was tiny; in fact, it had attracted only three other members: an Irish student named William Morgan, John Gambold, and Sally Kirkman's brother Robert. The aims of the club were simple: the members studied the classics and the Bible together on a Sunday night and attended Communion once a week at Oxford Cathedral. Even though everyone else involved in the Holy Club was younger than he, John was glad for the Christian fellowship and eagerly joined the group. Soon he was their leader—and reformer—and he decided that it would be good for the young men to follow his ideas regarding godly living. To this end, John added two more nights of study each week. He continued to add more meetings until the group was convening each night from six to nine o'clock.

All of these hours together gave the members of the Holy Club more than ample time to examine their own behavior as well as that of the other members of the group, according to a list of questions John gave them to review each day.

1. Have I embraced every probable opportunity for doing good and of preventing... evil?
2. Have I thought anything too dear to part with to serve my neighbor?
3. Have I spent an hour at least every day in speaking to someone?
4. Have I in speaking to a stranger explained what religion is not...and what it is, the recovery of the image of God?
5. Have I persuaded all I could to attend public prayers, sermons and sacraments?
6. Have I after every visit asked him who went with me: Did I say anything wrong?
7. Have I when someone asked my advice directed and exhorted him with all my power?
8. Have I rejoiced with and for my neighbor?
9. Has goodwill been...the spring of all my actions toward others?

Before long, other students at Oxford got ahold of this list of questions and began to mock the efforts of the members of the Holy Club. Sarcastically they called them Bible Moths, Bible Bigots, or Methodists. The name *Methodists* seemed to stick because the group appeared to have a method for everything. Someone even made up a rhyme about them.

By rule they eat, by rule they drink,
Do all things else by rule, but think—
Accuse their priests of loose behavior,
To get more in the laymen's favor;
Method alone must guide 'em all,
Whence Methodists themselves they call.

Despite the mocking of others, John and his followers in the Holy Club were undaunted. In fact, John was secretly pleased with the "persecution." It made him feel that he must be on the right track, since Jesus said, "Blessed are ye, when men shall revile you, and persecute you, and shall say all manner of evil against you falsely, for my sake" (Matthew 5:11). From time to time other young men joined the Holy Club, though its total number of members during the first year never grew past fifteen.

In early August 1730, William Morgan went to Oxford's Castle Prison to visit a man imprisoned for murdering his wife. At the overcrowded prison he discovered that debtor prisoners and general criminals, like the man he was visiting, were all locked up together. Although Castle Prison was dank and dirty, William was surprised at how the inmates were encouraged by his visit. Many of the prisoners had not had a single visitor since being locked up.

Following his visit, William told John and Charles about the situation at Castle Prison. The brothers were moved by his description of the conditions inside the jail and of the prisoners' hunger for comfort and contact with outsiders. Surely, William argued, such prisoners needed the comfort of the Christian message. John and Charles agreed, and on August 25, 1730, they accompanied William to Castle Prison.

John was deeply touched by what he saw in the jail and by how open the prisoners were to talking to him. In the process of these conversations, John learned that debtor prisoners were in jail basically for two reasons. Either they had been locked up because some misfortune had befallen them and their families, making it impossible for them to repay their debts, or they were locked up for not repaying their debts because of laziness or indifference. John was moved by the plight of the former and decided that perhaps the members of the Holy Club could pool their money to help pay the debts of some of these people or support their families while the men were locked up.

As usual, John wrote home to his parents, seeking their approval for his making regular visits to Castle Prison. To John's surprise, his father wrote back to say that he had also visited prisoners when a student at Oxford and that he thought it a fine and helpful activity for his sons to be involved in.

John was delighted by his father's response, and in his well-ordered, methodical way, he set up a schedule for the members to regularly visit Castle Prison. John wrote his name on the schedule to visit the jail each Sunday afternoon. As well, the club members began pooling their money and using it to minister to the needs of those prisoners they found deserving.

During the summer of 1731, Samuel and Susanna Wesley and their daughter Martha, along with two servants, were riding in a wagon when the horse pulling it bolted. The wagon lurched forward, and Samuel, who was sitting on a chair at the back, was thrown from the wagon. He landed on his head with a thud, and by the time the others got to him, he had stopped breathing and was turning blue. One of the servants managed to tilt Samuel's head back and get him breathing again, but the sixty-six-year-old man had suffered a serious injury.

When John heard about the accident, he was dismayed. Although he did not like to think about it, the accident reminded him that it was only a matter of time before his father would have to resign from his pulpit. What would happen then? John had the sinking feeling that his family would pressure him to take over the position and keep his mother and remaining single sisters on at the rectory in Epworth. This was not an appealing thought to John, and he tried to brush it aside.

Meanwhile John had problems of his own at Oxford. William Morgan was not well. No one could say exactly what was wrong with him, but he had rapidly begun to lose weight, and he slept little at night. Critics of the Methodists insisted that William had taken John's teachings on prayer and fasting too far, but John argued that no one could be too holy. While this debate raged back and forth, William's mental state deteriorated, until William was forced to return to Ireland in the hope that a change of air would do him some good. Unfortunately the change of air did little for him, and William died in August 1732.

John was deeply troubled by reports that William had suffered from religious hallucinations before he died and needed to be physically restrained for his own safety and the safety of those around him. John repeatedly prayed and asked God what had gone wrong, but he received no answer.

Things got worse for John when William's father wrote a bitter letter accusing him and the Methodists of being responsible for his son's death because of their extreme teachings and practices. When some at Oxford heard of the accusation that William's father had made in his letter, they took up his cause. As a result, John often had to endure being jeered at when he left his rooms at Lincoln College.

The jeering eventually died down, and in the summer of 1733 John became a member of the Society for Promoting Christian Knowledge, traveling to London from time to time to attend society meetings. During 1733 John met George Whitefield. George was a servitor (an undergraduate who performed menial tasks in exchange for financial assistance) at Pembroke College in Oxford. He admired the Holy Club and its members. John invited him to breakfast at Lincoln College, and the two men quickly became friends. In fact, they would become two of the most influential men of their era, and their lives would be entwined in various ways until their deaths.

The following year, 1734, started off with a wedding in the Wesley family. In January, Mary Wesley, who at thirty-nine years of age had given up all hope of marriage, found love in the form of the Reverend John Whitelamb. John was the acting curate under Samuel Wesley of the parish at Wroot. Unfortunately, John Wesley was not able to get away from his duties at Oxford to attend the wedding, but he was relieved to think that at least one of his sisters was happily married. Unfortunately, his sister's happiness was short-lived. Within a year of marriage Mary died in childbirth, along with the baby.

In January 1735, John received a sobering letter from his mother. "Your father is in a very bad state of health; he sleeps little and eats less. He seems not to have any appreciation of his approaching exit, but I fear he has but a short time to live," the letter read. It was time to face the future. Since Charles was not yet ordained, the opportunity—though neither of them thought of it as an opportunity—to take over their father's position as rector at Epworth fell either to John or his older brother Samuel.

By now Samuel had settled into the position of headmaster at the Tiverton Grammar School in Devon, and he did not want to move back to Epworth. He wrote to John and put pressure on him to help out the family by taking up the position. He suggested that since most students at Oxford considered John and the Methodists "strange," John might be better off with a fresh start somewhere else. John was infuriated that his older brother would try to plan his life for him, and he wrote a letter back to Samuel explaining why he should stay on at Oxford. Always an excellent debater, John used this skill to write a twenty-six-point rebuttal of his brother's argument for returning to Epworth and becoming rector. As to the matter of being strange and despised, he made the following points:

1. A Christian will be despised anywhere.
2. No one is a Christian until he is despised.
3. His being despised will not hinder his doing good, but much further it, by making him a better Christian.
4. Another can supply my place better at Epworth than at Oxford, and the good done here is of a far more diffusive nature, inasmuch as it is a more extensive benefit to sweeten the fountain than to do the same to particular streams.

In April 1735, Susanna sent out an urgent plea for her children to come home to Epworth to say good-bye to their father. John and Charles arrived at the rectory in time to gather at their father's bedside for one last blessing. John dreaded the moment, assuming that his father would put pressure on him to take the position as rector. But to his surprise, his father never mentioned it. Instead he turned to his son, his eyes bright, and said in a clear but frail voice, "The inward witness, son, the inward witness, is the strongest proof of Christianity." These were words that John would never forget. Nor would he forget the words his father imparted to Charles. "Be steady. The Christian faith shall surely revive in this kingdom, and you shall see it, though I shall not."

The Reverend Samuel Wesley was buried in the graveyard at St. Andrews Church, Epworth, on April 26, 1735. He had served the people of Epworth and the fens for over forty years, and none of his sons would take his place there as rector.

Following the funeral, the Wesley family home was broken up. Susanna went to live with Emilia, who was running a girl's boarding school in Gainsborough, while Kezziah, the only daughter still living at home, went to stay with Samuel and his wife, Ursula, in Tiverton. Meanwhile, John and Charles returned to Oxford via London to visit their sister Martha, who had gone to London to live with their uncle Matthew Wesley. Martha, however, had recently entered a hasty marriage to one of John and

Charles's friends, a staunch member of the Holy Club. The man's name was Westley Hall, and everyone assumed that the marriage would be strong and lasting. Unfortunately, it deteriorated instead in a scandal that affected the Wesley family and the entire church movement.

At thirty-two years old, John was no longer sure that he wanted to stay on as a fellow at Lincoln College in Oxford. Now that his father was dead and he was under no obligation to take up the position of rector at Epworth, John found himself at loose ends. As he searched about for what to do next, he visited Dr. John Burton, a professor at Corpus Christi College, Oxford. John had gotten to know Dr. Burton through his association with the Society for Promoting Christian Knowledge. Dr. Burton was one of the society's board members, and he was also a member of the board of trustees for the new colony recently established in Georgia in North America.

John explained to Dr. Burton what he was feeling. The doctor listened carefully to his words and then looked John in the eye and said, "I have just the man you should meet—James Oglethorpe."

John knew of James Oglethorpe by reputation. Oglethorpe was a former army general and a member of Parliament. As a member of Parliament, he had become concerned about the plight of debtors thrown into prison for failing to repay their debts. He found the whole notion of locking up debtors to be absurd. Not only were they forced to live in deplorable conditions in prison, but also, since they were locked up, they were cut off from any way of working to make money to discharge their debts. Oglethorpe had pushed for reform and eventually came up with the idea of establishing a colony on the strip of land situated on the coast of North America between Carolina to the north and Spanish Florida to the south. In so doing he would establish not only a buffer zone between the British and the Spanish in America but also a colony that would be a haven for debtors and for those fleeing religious persecution in Europe.

James Oglethorpe had presented his plan to Parliament, who endorsed it, and King George II had granted the new colony a charter. The charter was given to a board of trustees for twenty-one years and covered the land between the Savannah and Altamaha rivers and westward to the "South Sea." During this twenty-one-year proprietary period, the board of trustees (who were unofficially recognized as "governors") would make the colony's rules, though the liberties of Englishmen were guaranteed, as was the freedom of religion to all except Catholics. According to the charter, the purpose of the colony was threefold: (1) to afford an opportunity to the unfortunate poor to begin life over again, (2) to offer a refuge to the persecuted Protestants of Europe, and (3) to erect a military barrier between the Carolinas and Spanish Florida. At the end of the twenty-one-year proprietary period, control of the colony would pass to the British Crown.

The new colony was named Georgia, in honor of George II, and early in 1733 Governor James Oglethorpe and thirty-five families had set out for

Georgia. They sailed up the Savannah River in the spring of 1733, and on a bluff overlooking the river they founded a city, which they named Savannah after the river.

Dr. Burton explained that after two years in Georgia, Oglethorpe had returned to England to raise more money for the colony and to recruit more colonists, among them clergymen. John was about to make a trip to London to arrange for the publishing of his father's commentary on the book of Job, and Dr. Burton arranged for him to meet Oglethorpe while he was there.

James Oglethorpe was a strapping man with broad shoulders and a confident demeanor. He warmly greeted John and proceeded to tell him all about the Georgia colony. He explained how more and more people were arriving in the colony, including Pietists from Europe and Scottish Highlanders. As a result, the colony had an urgent need for qualified clergymen who could attend to the spiritual needs of the people. John, for his part, was intrigued by what he heard, but he was not sure whether colonial life was for him. Still, Oglethorpe seemed eager for him to come to Georgia and serve as vicar (a clergyman in charge of a chapel) in Savannah, and John promised to carefully consider the option.

Back in Oxford John could not settle down. The more he thought about it, the more he realized that it was time for a change, and the change James Oglethorpe seemed to be offering him became more appealing. While ministering to the spiritual needs of colonists in Savannah was what Oglethorpe had in mind for John, what really attracted him was the idea of converting the Indians, or "noble savages," as he referred to them, who also inhabited the Georgia colony. That, John decided, would be challenge enough for him.

John also had other, more personal reasons for going to Georgia, and he wrote them all down on paper:

> My chief motive to which all the rest are subordinate is the hope of saving my own soul. I hope to learn the true sense of the Gospel of Christ, by preaching it to the heathen. They have no comments to construe away the text, no vain philosophy to corrupt it, no luxurious, sensual, covetous, ambitious expounders to soften its unpleasing truths.... A right faith, will, I trust, by the mercy of God, open the way for a right practice, especially when most of those temptations are removed which here so easily beset me.

As he often did when faced with a decision, John wrote to his mother and to his brother Samuel, seeking their advice regarding a move to Georgia. Samuel was in favor of the idea, and Susanna wrote back a letter in which she said, "Had I twenty sons, I should rejoice that they were all so employed, though I should never see them more." John was also surprised to learn from his mother that shortly before his death his father had considered going as a clergyman to Georgia but eventually decided against the plan because of his age. His father had written to James Oglethorpe explaining, "Had it been but ten years ago, I would gladly have devoted the remainder of my life and labours to that place." John took this news as his father giving his support to the plan from beyond the grave.

John wrote to Dr. Burton and James Oglethorpe, offering himself as a clergyman to the Georgia colony, and the two men gladly accepted him to serve in Savannah. John did not intend to go to Georgia alone, however, and he set about recruiting several other young men to accompany him. Benjamin Ingham, who had been a member of the Holy Club in Oxford, agreed to go along, as did Charles Delamotte, the son of a London merchant and a friend of Benjamin's. John hoped to persuade one last person to go with him to Georgia—his brother Charles.

At first Charles rejected the idea. "Go with you to Georgia?" he exclaimed. "What possible use might I be to you there, since I am not yet ordained?"

Not willing to take no for an answer, John set to work on the situation. He managed to persuade the Bishop of London to ordain Charles, and he also secured for his brother the position of private secretary to James Oglethorpe. When he heard of the arrangements, Charles agreed to go.

Finally everything was in place, and in early October the four men made their way down the

Thames River to Gravesend, where the *Simmonds* was docked, waiting to set sail across the Atlantic Ocean.

As John climbed the gangplank to board the *Simmonds*, his chest swelled with confidence. *Surely,* he told himself, *God will use me to take the gospel to the noble savages.*

Nothing could have been further from the truth.

Chapter 7

Georgia

The *Simmonds* set sail for Georgia from Gravesend, England, on October 14, 1735. It was a red-letter day for John, who was on his way to a new start in a new land, a land that John hoped would take his mind off all earthly things and allow him to think only of God and His kingdom. John started off as he meant to continue, with a strict routine for himself and the other three men, for whom he took spiritual responsibility.

Each morning, John announced, the four men would all rise at four o'clock—any later was laziness—and pray privately for an hour. The next two hours, from five to seven, were to be spent reading the Bible together in the Wesley brothers' large cabin. Following this was breakfast with the other passengers, and then the next hour was to be spent in public prayer with any of the passengers who cared to join them. John would take close note of those who attended, since he was to become their pastor when they landed in Savannah. The rest of the morning was to be given over to study. Charles Wesley wanted to write sermons and spiritual poems, Charles Delamotte would study Greek, Benjamin Ingham chose to read theology or teach Bible stories to the children aboard, and John decided to learn German.

John was motivated to learn German mainly because accompanying the eighty English colonists aboard the *Simmonds* was a group of German-speaking Moravians. The Moravians were a Pietist group that had started in Moravia, a region of modern-day Czech Republic, and had suffered persecution there, especially at the hands of Catholic bishops. Many of them had fled to Germany, where Saxon Count Nicholas Ludwig von Zinzendorf had given them shelter on his estate at Herrnhut. The religious community they established had become zealous about sending out missionaries to foreign lands. In fact, the two Danish missionaries whose story Susanna Wesley had read to the people of Epworth back in 1712 had both been Moravians. A group of Moravians had already settled in Georgia, and this group aboard the *Simmonds* were on their way to join their brethren. None of the Moravians aboard spoke English, but John was eager to learn more about the people's theology and their church experience in Europe. Since the voyage to Georgia would last about four months, John was confident that he would be speaking German fluently by the time they arrived at their destination.

At noon the four Englishmen would again meet to discuss how well they had kept to their morning schedule and to plan the details of their afternoon before eating lunch at one o'clock. After lunch the men would spend the next four hours in private conversation with passengers about the spiritual state of their souls and teaching the children the Anglican catechism.

Two more hours of private prayer and group Bible reading were to follow, and then dinner, after which the men would join the Moravians for their hour-long prayer service. At eight o'clock in the evening they would again meet to account for how well they had followed their afternoon program and to search their souls for any doubts or rebellious thoughts. Then it would be off to bed at ten o'clock for six hours of sleep before starting the routine over again the next day.

As it had been in the past, food became an issue of holiness. John decided that the four of them should forgo the meat and wine served with the meals and live entirely on bread and water while aboard the *Simmonds.* Soon he felt that this regimen was not strict enough and declared that the four of them could also do without eating at all during the nightly dinner hour.

As the leader of the group, John felt compelled to hold himself to an even higher standard than the others. He tried to pray for the last five minutes of every hour he was awake, and he kept a diary examining every small detail of his feelings, faith, and actions. To ensure that this diary would never be read by anyone but himself, he devised and wrote in a complicated code. (His code was not deciphered until the 1930s.) John also prepared a public journal, which he hoped to publish at some later date. In his public journal he recorded the events that had the most profound effect on him during the long journey to Georgia.

> About one in the afternoon [Sunday, January 25, 1736] almost as soon as I had stepped out of the great cabin door, the sea did not break as usual, but came with full, smooth tide over the side of the ship. I was vaulted over with water in a moment, and so stunned that I scarce expected to lift up my head again till the sea should give up her dead. But, thanks to God, I received no hurt at all. About midnight the storm ceased.

The following day was worse, and John wrote,

> At four it was more violent than any we had had before. Now, indeed, we could say, "The waves of the sea were mighty, and raged horribly. They rose up to the heavens above, and clave down to hell beneath." The winds roared round us and—what I never heard

before—whistled as distinctly as if it had been a human voice. The ship not only rocked to and fro with the utmost violence, but shook and jarred with so unequal, grating a motion, that one could not but with great difficulty keep one's hold on anything, nor stand a moment without it. Every ten minutes came a shock against the stern or side of the ship, which one would think should dash the planks in a thousand pieces. In the height of the storm a child, privately baptized before, was brought to be publicly received by the Church.

Once he had performed the baptismal ceremony as best he could under the difficult circumstances, John went to the Moravians' cabin to see how they were faring. He was shocked by what he saw. They were in the middle of a church service, and John noted,

In the midst of the psalm wherewith their service began, the sea broke over, split the mainsail to pieces, covered the ship, and poured in between the decks, as if the great deep had already swallowed us up. A terrible screaming began among the English. The Germans looked up, and without intermission calmly sang on. I asked one of them afterward, "Was [sic] you not afraid?" He answered, "I thank God, no." I asked, "But

were not your women and children afraid?"
He replied mildly, "No, our women and children are not afraid to die."

As the *Simmonds* sailed on, the scenes he witnessed that day among the Moravians haunted John. Although he had preached countless sermons on trusting God and not being afraid of death, he had been as afraid as any of the other English passengers during the storm. Only the Moravians had been unwavering in their faith, believing that they were in God's will whether they lived or died. As much as John hated to admit it, he knew that he did not have that kind of total faith. In fact he was as afraid of death as anyone else on board. This realization shook him to the core, and he began to doubt that he was fit to be a missionary to the Indians, let alone a godly example to the English.

No one was more relieved than John when the *Simmonds* hove to off the lush coast of Georgia. The following morning, February 5, 1736, the ship crossed the bar and dropped anchor in the mouth of the Savannah River. The landscape was green and low-lying, made up of a number of islands packed close together. On the tip of one of the islands, which he soon learned was named Tybee, John observed a crude wooden lighthouse. James Oglethorpe informed him that he had ordered the structure to be built while he was away in England.

In his journal the next day, John wrote about a short but encouraging prayer service.

About eight in the morning, we first set foot on American ground. It was a small uninhabited island [Peeper Island], over against Tybee. Mr. Oglethorpe led us to a rising ground, where we all kneeled down to give thanks. He then took a boat for Savannah. When the rest of the people were come on shore, we called our little flock together for prayers. Several parts of the [lesson] were wonderfully suited to the occasion; in particular, the account of the courage and suffering of John the Baptist; our Lord's directions to the first Preachers of his Gospel, and their toiling at sea, and deliverance; with these comfortable words: "It is I, be not afraid."

Following the service on Peeper Island, most of those who had come ashore returned to the ship while Oglethorpe and several men traveled in one of the *Simmonds*'s boats upriver to Savannah for the night. What John did not record in his public journal was the situation he encountered when he returned to the *Simmonds*. John and Charles Wesley, Charles Delamotte, and Benjamin Ingham had stayed ashore on Peeper Island for several more hours to walk and talk. When they finally returned to the ship, John was stunned to discover that almost the entire complement of crew and passengers were drunk. Apparently a settler from the colony had rowed out to the *Simmonds* at anchor and smuggled aboard several barrels of rum, which by the time John arrived aboard ship had been drained of their contents. John could scarcely believe his eyes as people he thought were devout Christians stumbled about the deck drunk. Little could be done about the situation other than let everyone sleep off their inebriation.

The following day, when Oglethorpe returned from Savannah, John was still trying to reconcile what he had seen. The hungover passengers and crew were delighted to see Oglethorpe or, more precisely, the supplies he had brought back with him: beef, pork, venison, turkey, bread, and turnips—the first fresh food everyone aboard had seen in four months. The ship's cook, with the eager assistance of the women aboard, prepared a delicious meal, which was served on Peeper Island. John, though, stuck to eating bread and water, refusing to partake of any of the fresh, rich food.

Following the meal John decided to take a walk alone along the shoreline. As John walked, Bishop August Spangenberg, the leader of the Moravians in the colony who had accompanied Oglethorpe back to the ship from Savannah, fell in step beside him. John found himself in the company of a man who was as straight talking as he was. As the waves gently lapped at the sandy beach, Spangenberg leveled his blue eyes at John and instead of questioning him about the voyage across the Atlantic Ocean asked, "Does the Spirit of God bear witness with your spirit that you are a child of God?"

John felt his face turn red. He had no idea what to say.

Given John's silence, Spangenberg pressed on. "Do you know Jesus Christ?"

"I know He is the Savior of the world," John replied sheepishly.

"That is true, but do you know He has saved you?" quizzed the Moravian bishop.

"I hope He has died to save me," John said.

The short conversation left John feeling deeply unsettled, and he determined to spend more time with the Moravians and learn their secrets to living a holy life.

The following morning a flotilla of small boats came alongside the *Simmonds*, and soon passengers and cargo were being unloaded for the ten-mile trip upriver to Savannah.

Under orders from James Oglethorpe, when John arrived in Savannah, he took up his post as vicar. Meanwhile his brother Charles assumed his duties as Governor Oglethorpe's private secretary and accompanied Oglethorpe south to inspect the new settlement of Frederica. As the southernmost English settlement in North America, Frederica was the first line of defense against Spanish invasion from Florida.

John assumed that he would dive right into his missionary work among the Indians, but he was in for a shock. He was introduced to the Reverend Samuel Quincy, the man he was replacing. Mr. Quincy gave a look of surprise when John announced that he wanted to start learning the local Chocktaw Indian language as soon as possible. "That will not be necessary," Mr. Quincy said. "Your duty lies with the

English settlers. We must not interfere with the Indians. They could easily misinterpret what we are trying to do for them and go over to join the French or Spanish. Then we would have a serious situation."

John was speechless. He had been told that part of his duty as vicar would be evangelizing the Indians, or had he? Had that really been plainly spelled out to him in his conversations with Oglethorpe back in England, or had the impression that that is what he would be doing been given as a way of getting him to agree to sail across the Atlantic Ocean to Georgia? Whichever way it had happened, John felt cheated and betrayed. And such feelings were not a good foundation on which to build his ministry in this beautiful, new land he found himself in.

John moved into the parsonage (a house provided for a clergyman), but for the first few days he was so upset that he barely left the house. Then, resigned to his fate, he set out to visit his five hundred parishioners. Savannah was set on a bluff above the river. It had been meticulously planned with wide streets and squares at each intersection. Lining the streets were lots fifty feet wide and ninety feet deep on which sat houses. Many of the houses were the original 24-by-16-foot structures built of rough-hewn, unpainted wood. But many new, larger houses had also been built of planed wood painted white. Most of the lots were surrounded by picket fences. At the foot of the bluff, nestled beside the Savannah River, was a small fort armed with twenty cannons and manned around the clock by men from the community. Beyond the settlement were five-acre plots that each man in the community was given to grow produce for his family, and beyond these were the forty-five-acre farms each man was also allotted.

On March 7, 1736, John preached his first sermon in Savannah. In the course of delivering it, he outlined what he expected of the citizens of Savannah. Communion would be celebrated every Sunday and on special feast days, and no one who had not been baptized in the Church of England could partake. John also announced that anyone who wished to take Communion would have to give notice the day before so that he could assess the state of that person's soul. And finally he announced that he would not conduct funeral services for anyone who was not an Anglican and that the women should appear in church wearing plain, woolen or linen dresses. Those with jewelry or elaborate clothing styles should stay at home.

Such rigid rules, of course, gave John many instant enemies. One woman refused to allow her baby to be immersed in water three times (the common practice for baptism in the Church of England at the time), and another family grew incensed when John would not conduct the funeral service of their devout Dissenter father. Some of the colonists complained directly to James Oglethorpe about what they saw as John Wesley's heavy-handed approach, while others chose more subtle ways to get back at their new, strict and unbending minister.

Chapter 8

Escape

Governor James Oglethorpe decided to take up residence at Frederica, located on St. Simons Island seventy miles south of Savannah. This made it difficult for the residents of Savannah to complain about John's heavy-handed ways. And since he was the governor's private secretary, Charles Wesley also had taken up residence there. But things were not going well for Charles. He was not able to keep up with the paperwork his job entailed, and so Oglethorpe had relieved him of many of his private secretarial duties and assigned him a new responsibility. Since there was no vicar at Frederica, Oglethorpe had installed Charles in that position. But even in this new role, Charles was having problems.

Like his older brother, he instituted a strict code of conduct for the members of the church to follow. And just like the residents of Savannah, the residents of Frederica reacted negatively to Charles's rules for Christian living.

In particular, Ann Welch and Beata Hawkins, two of the women who had sailed over with Charles and John on the *Simmonds*, grew tired of listening to Charles and began a plot to get rid of him. Their plan was carried out in two parts. First, they went separately to Charles, and each of them told him that she had been Governor Oglethorpe's mistress. Then each woman went to the governor and said just the opposite—that she had been involved with Charles! Of course, Oglethorpe was as shocked as Charles at the allegations. The situation quickly devolved into a nightmare for Charles. No one knew who or what to believe about the situation, and Governor Oglethorpe held Charles responsible, regardless of whether he had done anything or not. In Oglethorpe's opinion, Charles had brought the whole situation on himself and the community by preaching such high standards of behavior that made life too difficult for the colonists.

Things continued to deteriorate in Frederica, and by the time John arrived to visit his brother, he found Charles sick and depressed. Unable to rouse Charles's spirits, John finally persuaded Governor Oglethorpe to allow his brother to return to England to personally deliver some important papers. In July 1736, Charles set sail from Georgia for England. He had been in the Georgia colony for less than six months and was never more pleased to leave a place in his entire life.

Despite the complaints he had heard about John and his heavy-handed ways in Savannah, James Oglethorpe took no action, and following the departure of his brother, John returned to his pastoral duties at Savannah. But he soon had a female problem of his own there. The problem came in the form of Sophia Hopkey, the eighteen-year-old niece of Tom Causton, the magistrate of Savannah. Sophia was a student at the school Charles Delamotte ran, and John tutored her there in French and religious studies. However, it was not long before John was visiting Sophia four times a day to supervise her schoolwork and walk with her in the myrtle woods while conversing with her in French.

John was probably the last person to admit it, but he had taken a great liking to Sophia. There was just one problem: he had taken his lead from St. Paul in the New Testament and had decided a long time ago that he would remain an unmarried minister. But Sophia was testing his resolve to the limit, and John had the strength neither to break off the relationship with her nor to tell her that he could not marry her. Eventually, in a state of torment, John sought out Johanns Toltschig, one of the Moravian pastors, to talk to about the situation. He asked if it was right for him to continue meeting alone with a certain young woman.

Johanns thought for a moment and then replied, "What do you fear might happen if you continue to meet with her?"

"I fear that I should marry her," John replied.

"I don't see what would be wrong with that!" the Moravian pastor exclaimed.

John shook his head. It was not the answer he had hoped to get, but as he thought about it, he realized that he was unsure of what answer he really wanted to hear. So John tried another tack. He confided in Charles Delamotte, who responded by suggesting that they draw lots, as the Moravians did, to see what God's will was in this instance. John agreed that this would be an acceptable approach, and Charles then took three slips of paper. On the first slip he wrote, "Think not [of marrying] this year." On the second slip he jotted, "Think of it no more," and on the third slip, "Marry." Charles then folded the slips of paper and placed them in a hat.

John reached cautiously into the hat and pulled out one of the slips of paper. He unfolded it and read, "Think of it no more." It may have been God's guidance to him, but deep down inside John was disappointed with the answer he had received. It was at that moment that he realized just how much he wanted to marry Sophia. But feelings aside, he believed that God had spoken to him and that he must do as guided.

Despite his best efforts, John found it nearly impossible not to think of Sophia. Savannah was a small, isolated village of about five hundred inhabitants, and John ran into Sophia just about everywhere he went. Finally, Sophia herself resolved the situation, or so it appeared at first. Sophia gave up on John and decided to marry a man named William Williamson, who was a boarder in her uncle's house. But while William was considered a good man throughout the community, as far as John Wesley was concerned, he was not good enough for Sophia Hopkey.

Perhaps sensing that their wedding would create trouble, William and Sophia decided to marry across the Savannah River in South Carolina. John heard of their marriage only after it had taken place, and he was infuriated, especially since the couple had not "posted banns of marriage" in Georgia. This meant that William and Sophia should have come to John, as their minister, to announce their intention to marry. Then for four consecutive Sundays, John would have read out the banns announcing the couple's intent of marriage, allowing time for anyone who knew of any reason why the two should not be married to come forward. Although this was not a legal requirement, it was common practice and was expected for Anglican weddings. John was annoyed that William and Sophia had gone behind his back, and as he tried to thank God for dealing with the situation he had gotten himself into with Sophia, he found himself too angry to give the newlyweds his blessing.

Naturally John's behavior upset Sophia, who in turn, along with William, stopped attending church regularly. John grew sick thinking about how he had let Sophia go. His bitter feelings over the marriage came to a head on August 6, 1737. Stating that she had tried to follow John's rules for holy living to the best of her ability, Sophia requested that she be allowed to take Holy Communion at the service the following day. But during the service, when Sophia came forward to the altar to receive Communion, John could not bring himself to administer it to her. Sophia was shamed by being refused Holy Communion in public, and her husband, William, was furious with John. He thought that John was trying to ruin his marriage to Sophia. John responded that he was merely a concerned pastor looking after a member of his flock.

The population of Savannah would have none of John's pastoral-care argument and came down firmly on the side of William and Sophia Williamson. Soon all of Savannah was in an uproar over the incident. Thomas Causton, Sophia's uncle, gathered complaints from disgruntled parishioners in town, and at seven o'clock in the morning of August 8, John answered a knock at the door. A constable handed him a document signed by Thomas Christie, the court recorder at Savannah. The document read,

Georgia, Savannah,
    To all Constables, Tithingmen and others, whom these may concern:
    You, and each of you, are hereby required to take the body of John Wesley, Clerk:
    And bring him before one of the bailiffs of the said town to answer the complaint of William Williamson and Sophia, his wife, for defaming the said Sophia, and refusing to administer to her the Sacrament of the Lord's

Supper, in the public congregation, without cause; by which the said William Williamson is damaged one thousand pounds sterling: And for so doing, this is your warrant, certifying what you are to do in the premises. Given under my hand and seal of the eighth day of August, Anno Domini 1737.

    Tho. Christie.

After reading the warrant, John pulled on his coat and followed the constable to the courthouse, where the charges against him were read. He was released without bail and admonished not to flee the colony. His court hearing was set for early December. Unfortunately for John, Governor Oglethorpe, the one man who might have been able to help him, was away in England.

As winter approached, John worried that he would never get a fair hearing in a court in Georgia—he had made too many enemies in the colony. Under the cover of darkness in the early hours of Saturday morning, December 2, 1737, John left the parsonage in Savannah behind for good. Skulking in the shadows he made his way to the banks of the Savannah River at a place where he could not be seen from the fort at the river's edge. Three men were waiting in a boat to aid John in his escape. They rowed him across the river to South Carolina. The plan, once they reached South Carolina, was to walk overland through the swamps and woods to Port Royal, where John and one of the other men, also escaping from Georgia, would board a ship headed for England.

Dawn was beginning to break as John and his companions set out through the thick forest. The men soon became disoriented and unable to tell which direction they were headed. They came upon a small cabin in which lived an old man named Benjamin Arieu. They stopped and asked Benjamin for directions to Port Royal, and Benjamin pointed to a narrow path.

"Follow the blazed trees, and they will take you to your destination," Benjamin said. (A tree had been "blazed" when a piece of its bark had been cut away to mark a trail.)

Soon the group were making good progress following the marked trees, that is, until midafternoon, when they came to a fork in the track, with blazed trees lining each fork. Not knowing which way to go, the group decided to follow the track that veered to the right. But after a mile, this track came to a sudden end in the middle of a dense stand of trees. The men could do nothing but turn around, retrace their footsteps, and follow the other fork of the track. This they did, but the other fork of the track also came to an abrupt end in the middle of a dense stand of trees. By that time the sun had begun to set, and the four men settled in to spend a cold night in the woods. Using a stick, they managed to dig down three feet to water so that they could drink, and John had brought a small cake with him, which he divided four ways.

Despite the difficult circumstances, John slept well on the damp ground, and as soon as the sun was up, the men began searching for the path to Port Royal. By midday they had not found it and decided to return to Benjamin Arieu's cabin. They arrived there just as darkness was descending. Benjamin was surprised that they had not been able to find their way and promised to send his nephew with them in the morning as a guide.

At sunup the next morning the group set out once again from Benjamin's cabin. It did not take the men long to learn that the old man's nephew was not very familiar with the path to Port Royal, and soon they were lost once again. Fortunately, the old man's nephew had a good sense of direction. When the track came to an end, he led the group on as they crashed through the dense forest and underbrush and sloshed over swampy ground. It took two more days, but eventually the group made it to Port Royal. John was glad to see the place, though his delight was tempered by the fact that no ships were anchored at the port, waiting to return to England. In fact, it was not until December 22 that John finally climbed aboard the *Samuel*, which had arrived several days before and was about to set to sea for England. The captain agreed to transport John home.

If John had hoped that his spirits would rise when he set sail from North America, he was sadly mistaken. He started the voyage with a bout of seasickness that subsided into a general depression. Thoughts of the high hopes he had had for himself when he had left England flooded his mind. He was going to be a missionary to the Indians, living a simple life and seeking God wholeheartedly. But what a mockery he had made of these intentions. He had hardly spoken to an Indian, had gotten caught up in all sorts of gossip, and had turned his life and Sophia's into a public spectacle. He had tried the best he could, and this was the mess he had managed to make of things. What good was he? Would he ever be able to do anything worthwhile for God?

To make matters worse, if that were possible, a storm blew up, and once again John feared for his life. This time there were no Moravians aboard ship to sing hymns with, and he felt as scared of dying as he ever had in his life. *Haven't I learned anything about trusting God in the last year and a half?* he asked himself. In the midst of his despair, John reached for his journal and wrote:

> I went to America to convert the Indians; but O! who shall convert me? Who, what is he that will deliver me from this evil heart of mischief? I have a fair summer of religion. I can talk well: nay, and believe myself, while no danger is near; but let death look me in the face, and my spirit is troubled. Nor can I say, "To die is gain!..." In a storm I think, "What if the Gospel is not true?" (Then I am of all men most foolish.)

The storm did not claim John's life or the *Samuel*, and as the vessel sailed on, John continued to pour out his heart in his journal.

It is now two years and almost four months since I left my native country, in order to teach the Georgia Indians the nature of Christianity: But what have I learned myself in the mean time? Why (what I least of all suspected), that I who went to America to convert others, was never myself converted to God. "I am not mad," though I thus speak; but "I speak the words of truth and soberness," if haply some of those who still dream may awake, and see, that as I am, so are they....

This, then, I have learned at the ends of the earth—that I "am fallen short of the glory of God"; that my whole heart is "altogether corrupt and abominable"; and, consequently, my whole life (seeing it cannot be, that an "evil tree" should "bring forth good fruit"): That "alienated" as I am from the life of God, I am a "child of wrath" and an heir of hell.

Christmas and then New Year 1738 passed aboard ship with little joy for John. As much as he hated being at sea, John dreaded the voyage's end in England. What would he tell his family and friends when he got there? And what would he do? Would he be accepted as a rector or curate now? He did not know, and he did not care.

Chapter 9

Saved by Faith

John disembarked at Deal in Kent, England, on February 1, 1738, more distraught and depressed than he had been when he embarked on the voyage in Port Royal, South Carolina. Once ashore, not wanting to face his friends in Oxford, John headed for London, where he stayed with his friend James Hutton. Upon reaching London, John was surprised to learn that a handful of small "Methodist" groups had sprung up around England. In the two years that John had been in Georgia, members of the Holy Club had taken up positions as ministers around the country and had spread the club's ideals. Even so, John did not take much pleasure in the spread of the club—he was preoccupied with his problems.

Six days after arriving back in England, John met a man named Peter Böhler. Peter was a Moravian en route to Savannah, Georgia, who needed somewhere to stay for a few days. Since Peter spoke no English and John spoke limited German, John offered to translate for him and help him find lodging during his stay in England.

It soon became apparent that Peter could help John a lot more than John could help Peter. The two men spent many hours talking about the state of John's soul and how exactly a person could be saved from hell and live a truly godly life. John put forward his best ideas, but Peter shook his head. "My brother, my brother," he sighed, "that philosophy of yours must be purged away." Sometimes John would agree with him, but other times he would argue the point.

Eventually, Peter and John visited Charles Wesley in Oxford. Charles questioned Peter closely and finally came to accept his assertion regarding a Christian being saved by the grace of God and nothing else. Charles's ready acceptance of Peter's message upset John. Although John wanted to believe what the Moravian said and tried hard to accept it, even after Peter talked and prayed with him, John felt that nothing had changed in his life.

When John finally asked Peter whether he should give up preaching altogether, the Moravian gave him a surprising answer. "Preach, brother, preach. I will not hear of you giving up."

"But what shall I preach?" John asked desperately.

"Preach faith till you have it; and then, because you have it, you will preach faith," Peter replied.

John decided to follow Peter's advice, and several days later he visited a condemned man at the local jail. As he walked into the prison, his mind was in turmoil. He wanted to tell the condemned prisoner that if he believed in Christ he would go to heaven when he died. But John wondered whether he could bring himself to do so. An instant conversion was far from anything he had ever taught before. After all, a person was supposed to demonstrate his or her conversion by doing "good works." If the condemned prisoner did convert, the man would not have the time or the freedom to show it by making any changes in his life, since he was to be hanged the next day. Still, John decided to go ahead. As he shared the gospel with the condemned man, both he and the prisoner became convinced that God's love was great enough to reach out even to a man who would not be able to perform any "works" after his conversion. John left the prison knowing that he was on the right track, though he did not feel that he had made the breakthrough he was waiting for.

The situation began to change for John on May 24, 1738. His day started out like many others, and John wrote in his journal.

I continued thus to seek it (though with strange indifference, dullness, and coldness, and unusually frequent relapses into sin), till Wednesday, May 24. I think it was about five this morning, that I opened my Testament on those words, "There are given unto us exceeding great and precious promises, even that ye should be partakers of the divine nature" [2 Peter 1:4]. Just as I went out, I opened it again on those words, "Thou art not far from the kingdom of God." In the afternoon I was asked to go to St. Paul's. The anthem was, "Out of the deep have I called unto thee, O Lord: Lord hear my voice. O let thine ears consider well the voice of my complaint. If thou, Lord, wilt be extreme to mark what is done amiss [wrongly], O Lord, who may abide it? For there is mercy with thee; therefore shalt thou be feared. O Israel, trust in the Lord: For with the Lord there is mercy, and with him is plenteous [plentiful] redemption. And He shall redeem Israel from all his sins."

The following day John's spiritual journey continued.

In the evening I went very unwillingly to a society in Aldersgate-Street, where one was reading Luther's preface to the Epistle to the Romans. About a quarter before nine, while he was describing the change which God works in the heart through faith in Christ, I felt my heart strangely warmed. I felt I did trust in Christ, Christ alone for salvation: And an assurance was given me, that he had taken away *my* sins, even *mine*, and saved *me* from the law of sin and death.

For the first time in a long while, John felt that he was truly a Christian and that his life pleased God. He wasted no time in telling others that they, too, needed to be "saved by faith." Most of the people who heard him speak thought that he had become unbalanced. James Hutton's mother even wrote to Samuel Wesley saying, "For after his behaviour on Sunday May 28th, when you hear it, you will think him not quite a right man.... John got up at our house and told the people that, five days before, he was not a Christian."

Samuel was not amused by the strange ramblings of his younger brother and wrote a sharp letter to John. "If you have not been a Christian ever since I knew you, you have been a great hypocrite, for you made us believe that you were one."

John soon found that his new theological position of being saved by faith offended many other people as well. He was banned from preaching at churches in and around London, and his friends were insulted by their conversations with him. Less than a month after his experience at Aldersgate, John felt under attack. He needed to go somewhere to sort out his feelings and decide what to do next. He soon settled on a destination: Herrnhut, in Saxony, the home of Count Zinzendorf and the Moravians.

On June 7, 1738, John visited his mother, who was now living with Anne in Salisbury. He explained to Susanna what had happened to him and how he intended to go to Germany, and then he asked for her blessing. But Susanna refused to give her son the blessing he sought. Instead she told John that she thought his new views were "extravagant and enthusiastic."

John set out for Saxony anyway, accompanied by his faithful friend Benjamin Ingham. After eight weeks of grueling travel, John and Benjamin reached the Moravian community in Marienborn, where John had learned that Count Zinzendorf was staying. John was so ill by the time he arrived that he managed only a brief conversation with the count. Although he felt under the weather, John was most impressed with the little he saw of the Moravian community. In his journal he wrote,

> The family at Marienborn consists of about ninety persons, gathered out of many nations. They live for the present in a large house hired by the Count, which is capable of receiving a far greater number; but are building one about three English miles off, on the top of a fruitful hill. "O how pleasant a thing it is for brethren to dwell together in unity!"

The following day John was feeling better, and he accompanied Count Zinzendorf on a short trip to visit a friend. John enjoyed observing the German customs and the people's interaction with one another at dinnertime.

At Marienborn John worked in the community garden and spent time talking with many of the Moravians. He found their message and their manners appealing, as he recorded in his journal.

> I lodged with one of the brethren at Eckershausen, an English mile from Marienborn, where I usually spent the day, chiefly in conversing with those who could speak either

Latin or English; not being able, for want of
more practice, to speak German readily. And
here I continually met with what I sought for,
[namely], living proofs of the power of faith:
Persons saved from inward as well as out-
ward sin, by "the love of God shed abroad in
their hearts"; and from all doubt and fear, by
the abiding witness of "the Holy Ghost given
unto them."

On Sunday, August 6, John was at Herrnhut,
where he joined in the religious services of the
Moravian community there. He found the services
refreshingly different.

After the Evening Service at Herrnhut was
ended, all the unmarried men (as is their cus-
tom) walked quite around the town, singing
praise with instruments of music; and then
on a small hill, at a little distance from it, cast-
ing themselves into a ring, joined in prayer.
Then they returned into the great Square, and,
a little after eleven, commended each other
to God.

John also attended the funeral service for a young
Moravian boy and was once again struck with the
simple faith he encountered.

A child was buried. The burying-ground
(called by them Gottes Acker, that is God's
ground) lies a few hundred yards out of the

town, under the side of a little wood. There are distinct Squares in it for married men and unmarried; for married and unmarried women; for male and female children, and for widows. The corpse was carried from the chapel.... They all sang as they went. Being come into the Square where the male children are buried, the men stood on two sides of it, the boys on the third, and the women and girls on the fourth. There they sang again: After which the Minister used (I think read) a short prayer and concluded with that blessing, "Unto God's gracious mercy and protection I commit you."

Seeing the [child's] father (a plain man, a tailor by trade) looking at the grave, I asked, "How do you find yourself?" He said, "Praised be the Lord, never better. He has taken the soul of my child to himself. I have seen, according to my desire, his body committed to holy ground. And I know that when it is raised again, both he and I shall be ever with the Lord."

All of these things impressed John, and John freely wrote about them. But other things disturbed him. One of these was the fact that Count Zinzendorf did not agree with Peter Böhler regarding the matter of being saved by faith. And because John still seemed to have many questions about his faith, the Moravians decided they would not allow him to share Communion with them, lest he "ate and drank

damnation upon himself." This insulted John, especially since they welcomed his friend Benjamin to
the Communion table.

John tried to look on the bright side of things,
and he spent some time visiting various Moravian
communities. When it was time for him to leave
Saxony and return to England, John wrote, "I would
gladly have spent my life here but my master [is]
calling me to labour in another part of his vine-
yard.... Oh when shall THIS Christianity cover the
earth as the waters cover the sea."

For the next several months John preached
wherever he was allowed to. His main sermon was
"By grace you are saved through faith." This was
not a popular message. John was seldom welcome
to preach twice in a church, and the Church of
England authorities were particularly worried by
the "strange enthusiasms" that gripped some of
those who heard his sermons.

For his part, John welcomed the idea that God
talked to His people in many different ways. He saw
nothing wrong with spiritual dreams, visions, and
supernatural voices. He took it in stride when, while
preaching at St. Thomas's Workhouse, a young
woman began crying out. She writhed around "rav-
ing mad, screaming and tormenting herself," as John
described it. John stopped preaching and prayed for
the woman, who immediately quieted down, causing many in the congregation to be moved to tears.

By the end of the year, John was allowed to preach
in only three or four Church of England pulpits. As a
result, he was unsure of how to proceed. Regardless,

the Methodists looked to him as their founder and unofficial leader, since the handful of small societies that had sprung up were direct descendants of the Holy Club in Oxford. John decided to spend New Year's Eve 1738–39 with a group of Methodists who met in Fetter Lane. The group planned a dinner of bread and water and an all-night prayer service. Seven members of the old Holy Club were present for the event, including George Whitefield, Charles Wesley, Benjamin Ingham, and John's brother-in-law, Westley Hall. About sixty other fervent Christians also were in attendance.

Later John described the event. "About three in the morning, as we were continuing instant in prayer, the power of God came mightily upon us, insomuch that many cried out for exceeding joy, and many fell to the ground. As soon as we were recovered a little from that awe and amazement at the presence of His majesty, we broke out with one voice, 'We praise Thee, O God, we acknowledge Thee to be the Lord!'"

It was George Whitefield and not John Wesley, however, who grasped the full spiritual significance of the night of prayer. The following day George wrote of the event, "We continued in fasting and prayer till three o'clock, and then parted with the conviction that God was to do great things among us."

It would be another three months before John would begin to experience what George had foretold.

Chapter 10

The World His Parish

As 1739 unfolded, doors continued to slam shut for John Wesley, as did they also for George Whitefield, who had turned out to be a fiery preacher himself. Finally, several members from the Methodist group at Fetter Lane suggested that George travel to Bristol and see whether there were any preaching opportunities there. Unfortunately, George's reputation as a fiery preacher had preceded him, and minister after minister in Bristol refused to have him in the pulpit to speak to their congregations.

Frustrated but not beaten by the situation, George declared, "I thought it might be doing the service of my Creator, who had a mountain for his pulpit and the heavens for his sounding board; and who, when his Gospel was refused by the Jews, sent His servants into the highways and hedges." So to the highways and hedges—or, more precisely, to the coalfields at Kingswood on the outskirts of Bristol—George went.

Kingswood was a spiritual no-man's-land in more ways than one. Since the Church of England was the official, state-sanctioned church, any new parishes had to be created by an act of Parliament. But the mining industry had sprung up quickly in response to England's growing industrialization, and no Anglican churches had been established in the area for the colliers (coal miners) to attend, not that they would have gone to such a church anyway. The miners were a crude and uneducated group who mocked any attempt to convert them to Christianity, that is, until George Whitefield arrived with his hard-hitting preaching style. The colliers and their families flocked to hear George speak in open-air meetings. Sometimes as many as twenty thousand people gathered to hear him preach!

John first heard of the events in Kingswood in a letter from George. The letter, written on March 3, 1739, described a "glorious door opened among the colliers of Kingswood." As he closed his letter, George invited John to "come and water what God has enabled me to plant."

A second letter from George, three weeks later, was more direct. "If the brethren [the Methodists at Fetter Lane], after prayer for direction, think it proper, prepare to arrive in Bristol at the latter end of the next week."

John was shocked when he read this second letter. George was seriously suggesting that he come to Bristol, preach in the open air, and train illiterate colliers in the way of the gospel. John did not want to go, and his brother Charles was even more opposed to the whole idea.

Still, the brothers decided that they should seek guidance from God as to what to do. Following the Moravian tradition, John prayed, opened his Bible, and pointed to a verse, which read, "With one blow I am about to take away from you the delight of your eyes. Yet do not lament or weep or shed any tears." Neither John nor Charles could say exactly what that meant, so they took the matter to the Fetter Lane Society. The members of the group suggested that John draw lots to settle the matter. John agreed, and he drew a slip of paper from a hat. The word written on the slip said, "Go," and without further questioning, John set out for Bristol.

When John arrived at his destination, conditions were worse than he had feared. By now George was preaching on a bowling green, and thousands of people were clamoring to hear him, climbing trees and sitting on rooftops for a better view. John shuddered at the thought of having to take part in such an unruly scene.

George was glad to see John and announced that he had decided to head for the Georgia colony. The next day he handed his preaching responsibilities over to John and set out on a final trip to London before setting sail for North America.

John shook his head in disbelief at the turn of events. He insisted that he could not preach outdoors. Instead he began preaching indoors to the small groups of Methodists who had rapidly sprung up in and around Bristol as a result of George's preaching. It was not long, however, before the Methodist meeting rooms were overflowing with people, and when the floor in one meeting place collapsed under the weight, John gave in and decided to preach outdoors.

Monday, April 2, was a day John Wesley would never forget. At three-thirty in the afternoon, John trudged over the slag heaps to the brickyard where he had agreed to preach. His stomach was in knots, and he tried not to think about what he, an ordained Anglican minister, was about to do. Although it was not illegal for him to preach outdoors, it was highly irregular and was frowned upon by the church authorities. John took a deep breath and prayed silently as a crowd of colliers who had just finished work for the day milled around him.

At four o'clock, John took another deep breath and launched into his first ever sermon delivered outdoors. He chose to preach on the text from Luke's Gospel: "The Spirit of the Lord is upon me, because he hath anointed me to preach the gospel to the poor; he hath sent me to heal the brokenhearted, to preach deliverance to the captives, and recovering of sight to the blind, to set at liberty them that are bruised, to preach the acceptable year of the Lord."

As John spoke, more and more people gathered to hear him, until the crowd numbered about three thousand. John preached on, feeling bolder as he went. When the sermon was over, he dismissed the crowd with a prayer and walked back to his lodgings.

That night he sat alone in his room, wondering how he had done. He knew he was not as dynamic a preacher as George Whitefield, but he had preached the gospel as best he knew how. Would it be enough? And would he have the courage to do it again?

The answer to these questions came the following day. John awoke singing a hymn and feeling that he was exactly on course with God's will for his life. He decided that later in the afternoon he would follow in George Whitefield's footsteps and go and preach at Hannam Mount, another coal-mining area just outside Bristol. But first, John was scheduled to speak at the Nicholas Street Methodist Society at 7:00 AM.

Even at that early hour, over one thousand people showed up to hear him preach. And that afternoon, when John finally made it to Hannam Mount, fifteen hundred miners stopped and listened to him preach. Later that night John walked on to Kingswood and Rose Green, where huge crowds gathered to hear him preach.

By the time he got to bed that night, John estimated that he had preached to over five thousand people! These were not just any people—they were people who had never attended a regular Anglican service and probably would not be welcomed there if they did.

More meetings followed, and strange events began taking place at them. Some of those who

came to hear him would shriek and writhe in agony
during the sermon as they came under conviction of
their sins. Others laughed hilariously or spoke in
"other tongues," or unknown languages, and could
not stop. John recorded many of the happenings
matter-of-factly in his journal.

April 21. At Weaver's Hall a young man suddenly was seized with violent trembling all
over and in a few moments sank to the
ground. We ceased not calling upon God till
He raised him up full of peace and joy.

May 21. In the evening I was interrupted at
Nicholas Street almost as soon as I had begun
to speak by the cries of one who was pricked
at heart and strongly groaned for pardon and
peace.... Another person dropped down,
close to one who was a strong assertor of the
contrary doctrine. While he stood astonished
at the sight, a little boy near him was seized
in the same manner. A young man who stood
up behind fixed his eyes on him and sank
down himself as one dead, but soon began to
roar out and beat himself against the ground,
so six men could scarcely hold him.

June 22. In the society one before me dropped
down as dead, and presently a second and a
third. Five others sank down in half an hour;
most of whom were in violent agonies. In

their trouble we called upon the Lord and He gave us an answer of peace.

Although such phenomena could be found in Anglican theology, such things were not a part of regular church practice, and as a result they drew a lot of criticism.

John was beyond caring, however. With George Whitefield's help he had uncovered his life's work—and he knew it. Millions of unchurched men, women, and children were waiting to hear the gospel, but no one in England had made an effort to bring it to them. John fully intended to be the one to preach the good news of Jesus Christ to them.

When his brother Samuel wrote complaining about some of the strange emotional outbursts that were accompanying his meetings, John wrote back, "God commands me to do good unto all men, to instruct the ignorant, reform the wicked, confirm the virtuous.... Men command me not to do it in another man's parish. That is, in effect, not to do it at all.... My extraordinary call is witnessed by the works of God.... I look upon the world as my parish."

Although the Methodists remained a group within the Church of England, the members of the group wanted to spend more time meeting together to pray and share each other's spiritual burdens. The two main Methodist groups in Bristol got together and decided to purchase their own meetinghouse. They called it simply "Our Room," and when they could not find the money they needed to pay off the building, John stepped in to help them out with the payments and renamed the place "The New Room."

A problem arose at the Fetter Lane Society in London. The members of this society had always leaned heavily toward Moravian teaching, as had John; but a preacher from Alsace, Philipp Henry Molther, arrived in London and began preaching at the meetings at Fetter Lane. Back when John had been experiencing doubts about his own salvation, Peter Böhler had admonished him to "preach until you have faith," but Molther gave the members of the Fetter Lane group the opposite advice. He called his new doctrine "stillness." And it meant exactly that. The Fetter Lane Methodists were told not to do anything at all unless they were one hundred percent sure that they were saved. This meant not going to church or fasting or praying or reading Scripture or attempting any good works.

When John returned to Fetter Lane after one of his visits to Bristol, he was horrified by what he found. Nine out of ten of the Fetter Lane followers were gone, staying away from society meetings for fear of breaking the "stillness" rule. All the charity work of the group had come to a halt, and almost no one was going to church to take Communion. Shocked, John determined to do something about the situation.

Doing something about the situation did not prove to be easy, however. Molther was a persuasive speaker, and many members of the Fetter Lane Society refused to listen to John as he pleaded with them, held special meetings among them, and wrote open letters to Molther. By July 1739 John felt that the cause was lost. He asked to speak one more time to the members of the Fetter Lane Society. Unable to reason with them yet again, he said, "I have warned you, hereof again and again and besought you to turn back to the law and testimony. I have borne with you long, hoping you would turn. But as I find you more and more confused in the error of your ways nothing remains but I shall give you up to God."

When John stood up to leave the meeting hall for the last time, twenty-five men and forty-eight women left with him. John knew that these people were his true followers and that he would have to find a new spiritual home for them.

Back in November 1738, John had preached twice at the site of the old Royal Foundry in Upper Moorfields, London. The foundry had once made cannons for the British military, but after an explosion in 1716, the site had been abandoned, and the workshop was relocated to Woolwich. Crowds numbering nearly six thousand had come to each of the services John preached at the site, and after one of the services, two influential men had encouraged John to purchase the old foundry as a site for a Methodist meeting hall.

Given the current circumstances, John decided that it was time to follow through with this plan. He arranged to lease the property, and soon those from the Fetter Lane Society and other Methodist societies in London were hard at work converting the run-down building on the site into a chapel and meeting rooms. When they were done, they would have a chapel that could seat fifteen hundred people, with men on one side and women on the other. The renovated building would also have another meeting room that could seat three hundred, and upstairs was a small apartment for John to live in.

By the fall of 1739, John was busier than ever, dividing his time between Bristol and the Methodist societies in London.

The winter that descended over England that year was one of the most severe in years. The Thames River froze solid, bone-chilling wind blew in from the North Sea, and cold rain saturated everything. Regardless of the weather, John toiled on, preaching outdoors. Often he found himself preaching in the dark, as night settled over the country at four-thirty in the afternoon during the winter. But neither the cold nor the dark seemed to keep people away. At one of John's meetings in Bradford, despite a torrential downpour, ten thousand people gathered outdoors to hear John preach.

During this time, Charles Wesley began to write hymns to be sung at these meetings. The purpose of the hymns was to get the Methodist point of view across. The catchy tunes and carefully crafted lyrics hopefully would stick in the minds of those who sang them or heard them sung and people would think about the meaning of the words throughout the day.

November 1739 brought with it bad news. Samuel Wesley died at the age of forty-nine. He had fallen ill during the night and died the following morning. John was shocked at the suddenness of his older brother's death and was distressed that Samuel had died believing that he and Charles were an embarrassment to the church. It was a bitter time, but John was determined to press on.

And press on John did. He experienced during this time a number of great high points, among them preaching to a crowd of fifteen thousand people and seeing many people healed and spiritually renewed through his ministry.

With the renovations at the old foundry now complete, John moved into his new upstairs apartment. He brought his mother, Susanna, who had become more open to his beliefs, to live with him there. John felt optimistic again. The Methodists now had permanent bases in Bristol and London. Now, John told himself, it was time to branch out to other cities across England.

Chapter 11

An Expanding Work

John and his followers were overly optimistic in thinking that things would go smoothly for them once they had their own meeting place in London. By the beginning of 1740, John's world was in an uproar. A disagreement between him and George Whitefield, recently returned from Georgia, had overflowed into a major theological clash. The two men disagreed over the age-old issue of whether God predestines, or chooses in advance, certain people to be saved or whether each person is free to make his or her own choice. For a while the two men agreed to disagree over the issue. But eventually John felt he had to stand up for what he believed. He wrote to George, saying, "There is blasphemy clearly contained in the horrible decree of preordination [or predestination]. And here I fix my foot. And on this I take issue with every assertion to it. You represent God as worse than the devil. But you say that you will prove it by scripture. Hold! It cannot do."

Charles Wesley also entered the fray, using his newly developed skills as a hymn writer to drive home his brother's position. In fact, Charles's hymns had become a popular tool for spreading John's belief that God had sent Jesus Christ to die for all people and that, because of this, no one was beyond the reach of Christ's salvation and love. In a time when most men and women could not read, the hymns were a powerful way to pass on ideas and seal them in the singer's memory.

And shall I, Lord, confine Thy love
As not to others free?
And may not every sinner prove
The grace that found out me?
Doom them an endless death to die
From which they could not flee
O Lord, Thine inmost bowels cry
Against this dire decree!

As the disagreement between John and George dragged on, the Bishop of London, Edmund Gibson, became furious that two Anglican ministers were stirring up dissent over such a complicated matter of theology. He ordered both John and George to appear before him, but neither man would do so. Both men claimed that they acted under authority from a power higher than a mere bishop and would not put themselves under the bishop's authority.

No doubt Bishop Gibson would also have dearly liked to discuss with John another issue—the matter of lay preachers. The Church of England was held together in part by strict observance of its rules. One of those rules made it clear that no man could preach unless he was ordained, and a man could not be ordained unless he had earned a degree from one of the church-approved colleges and pledged to uphold Anglican doctrine. The thought that anyone, a stonemason, farrier, or farmer, could stand and address a congregation on spiritual and theological matters was a shocking thought to the average Anglican. Yet it was an issue John was forced to grapple with, since in his preaching he encouraged men and women to speak openly with others about their faith.

The matter came to a head for John while he was in Bristol. He received word that a man named Thomas Maxwell had been preaching to the Methodists meeting in the converted foundry back in London. In fact, John was so alarmed by the news that he rushed home to confront Thomas. However, when he finally reached the foundry, his mother met him.

From the look on her son's face, Susanna could tell that he knew about Thomas's preaching. She offered him some advice. "John, take heed what you do with reference to that young man, for he is surely called to preach as you are," she said.

Her words stopped John in his tracks, and John decided to slip into the back of the meeting and listen to Thomas preach before confronting him. What John heard at that meeting astonished him. Although he was not a college graduate, Thomas Maxwell spoke with force and eloquence. For the first time, the idea that God could call any man to the pulpit to preach began to permeate John's thinking. John left the meeting shaken and told his mother, "It is the Lord's doing. Let Him do what seems good. What am I that I should withstand God?"

Despite theological differences, the Methodists began their first social program in the year 1740. As more and more landless peasants moved from the countryside into the towns and cities, poverty became more and more of a problem in England. John was troubled that the Methodists were not doing enough to help the poor. He arranged for part of the foundry to be turned into a small workshop, in which twelve poor members of the congregation were taught to card and spin cotton, a skill they could use to earn a living for themselves.

The presence of so many poor, unemployed people in the towns and cities created problems for the Methodists. With nothing else to do, many of these poor people banded together into roving groups, stealing, fighting, and generally making a nuisance of themselves. They particularly liked harassing people on the street, and here the Methodists made an easy target as they gathered in the open air for their meetings. These gangs would cluster around the Methodists to heckle and catcall and generally disrupt. Sometimes they would try to pick fights with people at the gatherings. On one occasion at Hampton in Gloucestershire, for an hour and a half a group of thugs poured hogwash, the scraps and swill fed to pigs, over a group of Methodists who had knelt to pray in the street.

John himself was not immune to such treatment. He was often harassed by unruly mobs when he stood to preach. Fortunately he was a powerful and persuasive public speaker, and on many occasions he was able to diffuse the situation through his preaching. Once, when John was preaching in the open air on a green at Pensford near Bristol, a group of thugs descended on the meeting. They brought with them a bull that they had spent hours baiting to make angry. They released the animal, hoping that it would charge into the crowd, causing mayhem and injuring some of those who had gathered to hear John preach. But the angry bull would not cooperate with its tormentors. Instead of charging into the crowd, the bull kept running around and around the outside of the group until it was so exhausted it could barely stand up. All the while John kept preaching.

Finally, in frustration, the rabble-rousers caught the tired bull and led it into the crowd. They pulled it to the front of the meeting to the table on which John was standing to preach. They then released it and tried to provoke it to attack John. Once again the bull failed to cooperate. It just stood in front of

John, snorting loudly. But when John saw that the gang of thugs was now angrier than the bull, he decided it was time to abandon the table. As soon as he did so, the group surged forward, grabbed the table, and took out their frustration on it, smashing it to matchwood.

Sometimes the local authorities tried to control the unruly situations when they developed, but more often than not they did nothing. And sometimes the anti-Methodist riots, as they came to be known, were stirred up by Church of England clergymen frustrated at and concerned by the growth of Methodism within their ranks. The anti-Methodist riots would last for several years.

October 1740 brought with it a shocking death. A prominent Methodist named William Seward, an associate of George Whitefield, had arrived back in England from the American colonies in March. William Seward was traveling around the country, preaching to people wherever a crowd would gather. And like other Methodist preachers, gangs of poor thugs often harassed him as he spoke. On one occasion he was pelted with rotten eggs. Then in the small town of Hay-on-Wye on the border of England and Wales, he was attacked by a mob. In the brawl he was struck over the head and died a short while later from a fractured skull, becoming the first Methodist martyr. His death had a deep impact on John Wesley and the other Methodist preachers.

Despite the persecution the Methodists faced in the streets, by the end of the year, John had organized a group of twenty lay preachers who had fanned out between Bristol and London to preach to the masses. Before these preachers set out, John outlined a set of rules to guide them:

1. Be diligent. Never be unemployed a minute....
2. Be serious.... Avoid all lightness, jesting.
3. Converse sparingly...with women, particularly with young women.
4. Take no step toward marriage, without first consulting your brethren.
5. Believe evil of no one....
6. Speak evil of no one....
7. Tell everyone what you think is wrong with him....
8. Do not [pretentiously act as] the gentleman....
9. Be ashamed of nothing but sin: not of fetching wood...or drawing water....
10. Be punctual. Do everything exactly on time....
11. It is not your business to preach so many times, and to take care of this or that society, but to save as many souls as you can....
12. Act in all things, not according to your own will, but as a son in the Gospel.

The lay preachers did their best to follow these rules, but in a number of the places they visited, they were not welcomed, especially when people realized they were not "qualified" to be ministers. One of the lay preachers, John Nelson, who was a stonecutter by trade, was mobbed and nearly beaten to death during an outdoor meeting.

The year 1741 brought little relief from troubles. Kezziah Wesley, John's youngest sibling, died suddenly. It was a bitter blow, as she was only thirty-two years old. Charles was especially crushed by her death, and Susanna Wesley also found it difficult to accept her daughter's passing.

Still, the work of sharing the gospel carried on. Then at the beginning of 1742, John discovered the secret to keeping the Methodist societies together. It happened in an unexpected way. In Bristol the Methodists were having difficulty raising the money needed to pay off their meetinghouse. Captain Foy, one of the wealthier members of the society there suggested that all Methodists pay a penny a week, if they were able to, until the meetinghouse debt was cleared. To make this happen, he advocated dividing the members of the society into groups of twelve, with one member taking on the responsibility of collecting the money. To show his support for the new plan, Captain Foy offered to form a group with eleven of the poorest society members and to pay each of their pennies if they were not able to.

The plan was an instant success, and soon the small groups were meeting together each week not only to donate their pennies but also to encourage and admonish one another. Everyone was enthusiastic about the new development, and John soon realized that in these small accountability groups lay the missing piece of Methodism. He immediately began encouraging the establishment of such groups everywhere he spoke. He even went so far as to allow the leaders of the groups to issue tickets of good conduct. These Methodist tickets were good for two months and were given to a member after he or she had paid a shilling entry fee. Any member who was absent from three consecutive meetings without a good excuse was not issued another ticket and was no longer considered a Methodist. The system was simple and easy to administer, freeing John to take on preaching assignments farther afield.

Two months later, Lady Huntingdon, a financial supporter of both John Wesley and George Whitefield, suggested that John take his straightforward gospel message to the colliers in the north of England. Since he now had his Methodist groups in Bristol and London under control, John decided to take her advice to go north. He took with him John Taylor, one of Lady Huntingdon's servants, who was also a lay preacher. The two men rode their horses north to Newcastle, arriving there on May 30, 1742.

Since they did not know anyone in Newcastle, the two men had to think of a way to draw a crowd. This proved easy for John. He found his way to the hillside slum of Sandgate, where he and John Taylor stood on a busy street corner. Amid the hustle of vendors and shoppers, they began to sing a hymn. A small crowd of curious onlookers gathered to see what they were up to. Soon more people joined the crowd until, in a short time, several hundred people were peering over each other to see what the attraction was. When John judged the moment to be right, he began preaching to the gathered throng, using the text, "He was wounded for our transgressions."

At the end of the sermon, John Wesley invited the listeners back to hear him preach that evening. This time the crowd was bigger, and John began to hold regular preaching and teaching sessions at Sandgate. Within two weeks he had attracted a core group of men and women who were ready to be organized into small groups. John Wesley and John Taylor worked tirelessly to make sure the Newcastle Methodists were a united group. To ensure this, they broke ground on an orphan house—a project that everyone could contribute something toward and that would help the young and the destitute of the slum. After this, the two preachers headed south again, pleased with the progress of the new Methodists.

It had been seven years since John had visited his childhood home in Epworth, and he decided to make a side trip there on the journey back to London. He stayed at a local inn in Epworth, where he met a woman who had been a Wesley family servant many years before. The woman was overjoyed to see John again and asked him if he would be preaching in his father's old church the following Sunday. John had to admit that he did not know—he would like to, but his Methodist ideals had slammed many church doors shut to him. However, emboldened by the enthusiastic welcome of the woman, John walked to the rectory, where he talked with the curate, the Reverend Romley. Mr. Romley gave John a frosty welcome and assured him that no help was needed in the church. John shrugged off the insult and determined to at least attend the dinner-hour prayer service that evening.

It felt strange to John to be back at St. Andrews Church. The church held so many memories for him. John could hear his father's voice booming from the pulpit and imagine his mother and brothers and sisters all sitting side by side in the front row. But now his brother Samuel and his sisters Mary and Kezziah were dead. John thought about the time when his father was away in London and his mother had started holding unofficial meetings in the rectory kitchen, reading aloud the account of the first two European missionaries to India. What an impact those meetings had had not only on the members of St. Andrews but also on the residents of Epworth and the fens. In a sense, his mother's meetings were the forerunner to the Methodist societies that were springing up around the country. John looked forward to getting back to London to see his mother and tell her all about Epworth.

The Reverend Romley opened the prayer service with the text, "Quench not the Spirit." And then, looking straight at John, he launched into a scathing attack on ungodly people with "enthusiasms." There was no doubt in anyone's mind that the speech was a warning against associating with the old rector's radical son.

The congregation milled around the churchyard following the prayer service, unwilling to go home until they had heard from John Wesley. John Taylor seized the moment by announcing, "Mr. Wesley, not being permitted to preach in the church, will preach here in the churchyard at six o'clock."

A ripple of excitement went through the crowd, and John knew that he would have a large audience at that hour. Sure enough, at six o'clock he stood on his father's tombstone and began to preach to the large crowd that had gathered to hear him. "The kingdom of heaven is not meat and drink; but righteousness, and peace, and joy in the Holy Ghost," he began.

When John had finished preaching, many people lingered to hear from him about how to be saved and forgiven of their sins.

John was so pleased by the outcome of the meeting that he decided to stay on in Epworth for another week. The following Saturday he recorded in his journal the events of the day's open-air meeting.

I preached on the righteousness of the Law and the righteousness of faith. While I was speaking, several dropped down as dead; and among the rest, such a cry was heard, of sinners groaning for the righteousness of faith, as almost drowned my voice. But many of these soon lifted up their heads with joy, and broke out into thanksgiving; being assured they now had the desire of their soul—the forgiveness of their sins.

I observed a gentleman there, who was remarkable for not pretending to be of any religion at all. I was informed that he had not been at pubic worship of any kind for upwards of thirty years. Seeing him stand as motionless as a statue, I asked him abruptly, "Sir, are you a sinner?" He replied, with a deep and broken voice, "Sinner enough," and continued staring upwards till his wife and a servant or two, who were all in tears, put him into his chaise [a horse-drawn carriage] and carried him home.

On Sunday, June 13, 1742, John preached for the last time at the Epworth churchyard. He was deeply moved to see that so many people had accepted his message.

At six…I preached to a vast multitude gathered together from all parts, on the beginning of our Lord's Sermon on the Mount. I continued among them for near three hours; and yet we scarce knew how to part. O let none think his labour of love is lost because the fruit does not immediately appear! Near forty years did my father labour here; but he saw little fruit for all his labour. I took some pains among this people too; and my strength also seemed spent in vain. But now the fruit appeared. There were scarce any in town on whom either my father or I had taken any pains formerly, but the seed, sown so long since, now sprung up, bringing forth repentance and remission of sins.

As John Wesley and John Taylor rode on to London via Bristol, they were in high spirits. Their itinerating trip had been more successful than they could have hoped. John was particularly excited about giving his mother an account of his time in Epworth. He knew she had given so much of her life to the work there, and he felt sure that she would be deeply moved to know that the Wesley family's efforts had borne spiritual fruit.

What John did not know was that he would have to ride swiftly if he wanted to see his mother alive again.

Chapter 12

Refining the Rules

Friday, July 23, 1742, was a day John Wesley would never forget. He struggled with the words to describe it as he wrote in his journal:

About three in the afternoon I went to see my mother, and found her change was near. I sat down on the bedside. She was in her last conflict; unable to speak, but I believe quite conscious. Her look was calm and serene, and her eyes fixed upward, while we commended her soul to God. From three to four, the silver cord was loosing, and the wheel breaking at the cistern; and then, without any struggle, or sigh, or groan, the soul was set at liberty. We stood round the bed and fulfilled her last request, uttered a little before she lost her speech: "Children, as soon as I am released, sing a psalm of praise to God."

Two days later, John led the funeral service for his mother, and then Susanna Wesley was buried beside her parents in the Dissenters' cemetery at Bunhill Fields, adjacent to the foundry. In his journal John recorded the day as follows:

Sunday, August 1. Almost an innumerable company of people being gathered together, about five in the afternoon, I committed to the earth the body of my mother, to sleep with her fathers. The portion of Scripture from which I afterward spoke was, "I saw a great white throne, and him that sat on it, from whose face the earth and the heaven fled away; and there was found no place for them. And I saw the dead, small and great, stand before God; and the books were opened: And the dead were judged out of those things which were written in the books, according to their works." It was one of the most solemn assemblies I ever saw, or expect to see on this side of eternity.

For his mother Charles Wesley composed the poem that was engraved on her tombstone:

Here lies the body
of
Mrs. Susanna Wesley,

The youngest and the last surviving
  daughter of
Dr. Samuel Annesley
In sure and steadfast hope to rise,
And claim her mansion in the skies,
A Christian here her flesh laid down,
The cross exchanging for a crown...

John mourned the death of his mother. Susanna had been his confidante and spiritual adviser his whole life, and he valued her opinions above all others. But now she was gone, and John had to go on alone. In his grief he threw himself into his work with even more vigor. Some days he would ride up to fifty miles on horseback and preach five sermons. His plan was to strengthen the Methodist societies within the triangular area marked by Newcastle in the north, Bristol in the southwest, and London in the southeast.

It was not an easy task. John faced opposition from many Church of England clergymen and the congregations they stirred up against him. Persecution became a way of life to John. He was stoned twice, pelted with manure, and hounded when he conducted outdoor meetings. Sometimes the church bells in a town or village were rung nonstop in an attempt to drown out John's voice as he preached.

In January of 1743, as John was riding to Newcastle, he felt that God wanted him to purge out any Methodist society members who were not living out the truth of the gospel. When he arrived in Newcastle, he called together the Methodist leaders there and asked them to give an account of those under them. As a result, sixty-four members of the society were expelled, including seventeen for drunkenness, four for "evil speaking," two for cursing and swearing, and one for violence.

When it was over, John decided that it was time to write a formal constitution for the Methodist societies so that the members of each society would have a clear idea of what was and was not acceptable behavior. The document he wrote was called *The Nature, Design and General Rules of the United Societies.* In the document he explained how men and women were to act if they wanted to continue to call themselves Methodists:

There are about twelve persons in every class; one of whom is styled *the Leader.* It is his business, (1) To see each person in his class once a week at least, in order to inquire how their souls prosper; to advise, reprove, comfort, or exhort, as occasion may require; to receive what they are willing to give toward the relief of the poor. (2) To meet the Minister and the Stewards of the society once a week; in order to inform the Minister of any that are sick, or of any that walk disorderly, and will not be reproved; to pay to the Stewards what they have received of their several classes in the week preceding; and to show their account of what each person has contributed....

It is therefore expected of all who continue therein, that they should continue to
evidence their desire of salvation,

First: By doing no harm, by avoiding evil
in every kind; especially that which is most
generally practiced: Such as, the taking the
name of God in vain; the profaning the day
of the Lord, either by doing ordinary work
thereon, or by buying or selling; drunkenness,
buying or selling spirituous liquors, or drinking them, unless in cases of extreme neces-
sity; fighting, quarreling, brawling; brother
going to law with brother; returning evil for
evil, or railing for railing; the using of many
words in buying or selling; the buying or selling unaccustomed goods; the giving or taking things on usury, that is, unlawful interest;
uncharitable or unprofitable conversation,
particularly speaking evil of Magistrates or
of Ministers; doing to others as we would
not they should do unto us; doing what we
know is not for the glory of God, as the
"putting on of gold or costly apparel"; the
taking such diversions as cannot be used in
the name of the Lord Jesus; the singing those
songs, or reading those books, which do not
tend to the knowledge or love of God; soft-
ness, and needless self-indulgence; laying up
treasures upon earth; borrowing without a
probability of paying; or taking up goods
without a probability of paying for them.

It is expected of all who continue in these societies, that they should continue to evidence their desire of salvation;

Secondly: By doing good, by being, in every kind, merciful after their power; as they have opportunity, doing good of every possible sort, and as far as is possible, to all men;—to their bodies, of the ability which God giveth, by giving food to the hungry, by clothing the naked, by visiting or helping them that are sick, or in prison...;

Thirdly: By attending upon all the ordinances of God. Such are, the public worship of God; the ministry of the word, either read or expounded; the supper of the Lord; family and private prayer; searching the Scriptures; and fasting, or abstinence.

JOHN WESLEY, CHARLES WESLEY.
May 1, 1743.

With the establishing of this constitution, the number of people wanting to belong to the Methodist societies continued to grow, as did the opposition to the societies. In the summer of 1743, the situation was particularly dangerous for the groups in central England. In Swindon the volunteer fire brigade turned their hoses on those attending an outdoor meeting, and in other places, Methodists meeting together were pelted with everything from hogwash to rotten vegetables and eggs. And by fall anti-Methodist riots were breaking out in Staffordshire.

John decided he needed to travel around and support the beleaguered societies. He arrived in the town of Wednesbury near Manchester on Thursday, October 20, 1743, to find that rioters had damaged more than eighty houses belonging to members of the local Methodist society. News that John Wesley, the founder of Methodism, was in the area spread like wildfire.

John preached to a group of Methodists in Wednesbury and then retired to the house of Francis Ward, one of the local Methodists. At about five in the afternoon a mob of three hundred people descended on the place and surrounded it, demanding that John come out of the house. When John did come out, he spoke to the mob for several minutes, and the mob's anger seemed to subside. Finally John and the leaders of the mob agreed to go together to visit the local magistrate and talk the situation over with him.

The magistrate, Mr. Lane, lived at Bentley-Hall, two miles from Wednesbury. John led the way, with the mob falling in behind. When they arrived at Mr. Lane's house, it was well after dark, and Mr. Lane had retired for the night. His refusal to be roused from his bed when the group arrived at his front door revived the mob's anger, and the angry mob decided to march John on to the town of Walsal to see another judge. When they reached Walsal, a mob from that town joined those from Wednesbury, and an ugly situation quickly developed. A number of people began to call for John's life, and as people became more and more physical, John began to fear that they would follow through on the call.

Finally, near the middle of town, exhausted, John raised his voice and yelled, "Are you willing to hear me speak?"

"No, no!" many in the mob yelled back. "Knock his brains out. Down with him. Kill him."

Despite the mob's call for his death, John raised his voice once more and addressed the mob. "What evil have I done? Which of you all have I wronged in word or deed?" John continued speaking for fifteen minutes, urging the crowd to search their hearts and think about what they were doing. Then he ended with a prayer.

When he stepped down from the chair he had stood on to speak, one of the leaders of the mob was so moved by John's words that he said, "Sir, I will spend my life for you. Follow me, and not one soul here shall touch a hair of your head."

Three other men stepped forward and offered to help ferry John from danger. The four men stood in front and behind and on either side of John. As they all walked forward, the crowd parted in silence and let them through. The men guided John safely back to Francis Ward's house in Wednesbury at well after midnight. John thanked the men for their effort on his behalf and invited them to attend one of his meetings the following day.

In the face of such persecution, John pressed on, encouraged by the growing number of followers who continued to join the Methodist societies.

Then in February 1744, religious intolerance in England reached a new level. The British feared that Catholic France was planning to launch an attack against them. In response to this fear, all English Catholics were ordered to leave London, because it was thought that they might aid the enemy. Knowing how the leaders within the Church of England viewed Methodists, John rushed to reassure King George that he and all of the Methodists were loyal to the English crown.

Later that same year, John decided it was time to call all of the Methodist leaders together to decide how to proceed with the societies. From June 25 to June 30, 1744, Methodist leaders gathered for the conference at the foundry chapel in London. The topics John hoped to cover during the conference were church discipline, organization, union with the Moravians, and rules for "assistants." This last point proved to be the most controversial. Until this time, John and Charles Wesley had allowed unordained, or lay, preachers, but they had not actively promoted them within the societies. But this was about to change. John used his influence to make lay preaching a cornerstone of Methodism. Scoffers remarked that some of the men John promoted were "much fitter to make a pulpit than to preach in one," but John shrugged off such criticism.

The duties and obligations of these lay preachers were spelled out in great detail. The preachers were to travel around preaching to the greatest crowds possible, and they were to form societies to encourage the ongoing spiritual development of their converts. They were to do whatever was needed to sustain themselves along the way. John instructed his preachers, in contrast to most Church of England clergymen, to "be ashamed of nothing," willingly and cheerfully carrying wood, drawing water, or cleaning shoes. And these preachers, like John Wesley himself, were to eat simple meals, though John did not require them to become vegetarians, as he had in recent years.

When it was over, the conference at the foundry chapel was declared a great success, and another one was planned for the same dates the next year. Following the gathering John found himself invigorated by the possibilities that lay ahead, and he immediately set off on a long preaching tour.

On September 18, 1745, John arrived in Newcastle on one of his regular visits to the city. September 18 was also the day that Charles Stuart (known as Bonnie Prince Charlie, or the Young Pretender) and a band of fighters he had recruited from the Scottish Highlands overran and occupied Edinburgh. This was the first step in the prince's campaign to return the Catholic Stuarts to the thrones of England and Scotland. From Edinburgh Charles intended to push south across the border into England and march on to London to depose King George II and install himself king, in turn bringing England back into the Catholic fold.

When news of the capture of Edinburgh reached Newcastle, fear gripped the town. After all, Edinburgh was only ninety miles north of Newcastle. Immediately the city sprang into action to defend itself against attack. Militias were established, cannons were set on the city wall, and several gates in that wall were bricked up. As well, the men in the city were called by the mayor to swear loyalty to King George, which John Wesley was happy to do.

Fearing the impending invasion, many people in and around Newcastle fled south. But John stayed put in the Methodist orphan house, which was located on a rise just outside the city wall. There he intended to pray for an English victory in the fighting and encourage the local Methodists. He had complete trust in God, knowing that he was in God's will whether he lived or died.

Everyone in Newcastle breathed a sigh of relief when, after several weeks, the threatened attack did not come. Instead Charles Stuart and his Scottish fighters bypassed Newcastle as they pushed south into England.

Chapter 13

Partnerships

By the end of November 1745, John felt that things were safe enough in Newcastle for him to leave the Methodist work there in the hands of lay workers. One woman in particular, a young widow named Grace Murray, had greatly impressed John with her ability. John chose her to take charge of the orphan house.

With things settled in Newcastle, John climbed onto his horse for the ride south to London. The slow journey was interrupted almost hourly by watchmen who wanted to be sure that he was not a Scottish spy. The watchmen's fears were justified. The Scottish army had begun to sweep down into the English Midlands. However, English forces had managed to beat them back. The Duke of Cumberland, with a nine-thousand-man army, then chased Charles Stuart and his army all the way back to Scotland, where on April 16, 1746, at Culloden Moor, one last pitched battle was fought. The battle ended badly for the Scots. While three hundred Englishmen were killed in the fighting, two thousand Scottish fighters perished. Charles Stuart managed to escape the battlefield alive and went into hiding in the Scottish Isles before finally escaping to France. Following the defeat of the Scots, an uneasy peace descended over the British Isles.

John was delighted when the fighting was finally over. He hoped and prayed that it would help to end the ongoing persecution and harassment of the Methodists.

In the meantime John had decided that it was time to wage his own inner battle with, of all things, drinking black tea. In eighteenth-century England, tea was an expensive beverage, costing sixty shillings for a pound of tea leaves. John felt that this price was just too high for him to justify continuing to drink tea. Besides, tea seemed to make his hands shaky. John decided to set a good example for his followers by not spending any more money on tea and by not drinking tea when it was offered to him.

"I considered what an advantage it would be to these poor enfeebled persons if I would leave off what so manifestly impairs their health and thereby hurts their business also. If they used English herbs instead of tea, they might hereby not only lessen their pain but in some degree their poverty," John wrote of his decision.

Overcoming his desire to drink black tea spurred John on, and he decided to write a book about healthy living. He called it *An Easy and Natural Method of Curing Most Diseases.* In the book he described 243 diseases and listed over 700 cures for them. His emphasis was on healthy living and simple cures: cold baths, hot poultices, herb teas, and attention to personal hygiene and clean surroundings were his standard treatments.

John also opened the "People's Dispensary" at the foundry. This was a clinic where poor people could visit a doctor and receive medicine. The clinic was popular from the start, with a steady stream of patients lining up to see the doctor each day. Such a successful ministry convinced John more than ever that God was interested in the health of all men and women. With this thought in mind, John gathered up his new book on health and again took to the road. He wanted every Methodist to read the book and follow his health advice. Rain, hail, sleet, or snow would not deter him in this effort. If he thought conditions were too harsh for his horse, he would leave the animal in the barn and set out on foot.

John also developed other ways to help the very poorest people. During a stop at Kingswood near Bristol, he agreed to take over the running of a school for the sons of miners. His decision to do so spurred him to open a school for the sons of Methodist preachers in the hope of educating a new generation of Methodists. Soon the two schools, a day school for miners' sons and a boarding school for preachers' sons, were running side by side at Kingwood.

During 1746 John started a fund to give loans to poor Methodists. The loans were for one pound per person and were to be paid back over a three-month period. Like the health clinic, the loan program was very popular, and in its first eighteen months of operation, 225 people were helped by these short-term loans.

John also encouraged everyone to reach out to and help the poor. In a revised set of rules for Methodist leaders, he wrote,

> If you cannot relieve, do not grieve, the poor: Give them soft words, if nothing else: Abstain from either sour looks, or harsh words. Let them be glad to come, even though they should go empty away. Put yourself in the place of every poor man; and deal with him as you would God should deal with you.

By the summer of 1747 John was feeling a new call—Ireland. John traveled to Dublin, where he found that a Methodist work was already under way. The work had been started several years earlier when George Whitefield stopped off in Dublin on his way to the American colonies. The Dublin Methodist society already had 280 members, and John was impressed with their teachable attitudes.

When John returned to London from Ireland, he learned that Westley Hall had run off to the Caribbean and had left Martha and their children. John could do nothing about the situation but take in Martha and the children to live with him. Now he and Charles were together supporting their sisters Martha, Susanna, and Emilia. The Wesley women all embraced the Methodist movement and became strong helpers to their brothers.

In late 1747 Charles found an even better helper— a potential wife. Her name was Sally Gwynne, and although she was only twenty-three years old, Charles, who was now forty, felt that the two of them made an excellent couple. He even wrote her a love poem:

Two are far better than one
For counsel or for fight
How can one be warm alone
Or serve his God aright?

This question "How can one be warm alone, or serve his God aright?" was a strange question coming from a Wesley brother. Both John and Charles had sworn off marriage, and both brothers agreed that a man could serve God better as a single person than as a married man. In fact, they had made a pact together never to marry without the other brother's permission, a pact that Charles stretched to the limits when he introduced Sally to John.

John was not impressed with his potential sister-in-law and promptly drew up a list of more suitable candidates for Charles if he insisted on marrying someone. Having drawn up the list, he gave it to Charles and then left for a trip north, not knowing that his opinion about marriage was about to change, as had Charles's.

In July 1748 John was in Newcastle when he fell ill with a migraine headache. As the keeper of the orphan house there, Grace Murray, nursed him back to health, John began to take an interest in her. She was thirty-two years old, thirteen years younger than John, a pretty and pious widow, and one of the most respected Methodist women in the Newcastle area.

Soon John was entertaining the idea of marriage for himself. He invited Grace to accompany him the following year on a second trip to Ireland so that she could help by encouraging other Methodist women. At the beginning of April 1749, John and Grace set out on their journey. Their first stop was in Wales, where Charles Wesley was at the time. Charles still believed that it was God's will for him to marry Sally Gwynne, and John had since come to this understanding as well. In Garth, Wales, on April 8, 1749, John Wesley officiated at the wedding of Charles and Sally.

John and Grace then traveled to Ireland. After seeing how happy his brother was following the wedding, John wanted to pursue marriage with Grace. But this was difficult for him. Although he spent countless hours with Grace on their tour of Ireland, he lacked the courage to have an open conversation with her about his intentions. Most of the time that she was with John, Grace thought that he viewed her as an admirable colaborer in the Methodist work, although John did manage to tell her, "If ever I marry, I think you will be the person."

Unfortunately for John Wesley, another Methodist preacher, John Bennet, also thought that Grace Murray would make a suitable wife, and he set to wooing her. The entire situation was soon out of control, with both John Wesley and John Bennet assuming they were engaged to Grace.

To make matters worse, John hid the relationship from Charles, even though he and Charles had made a pact to share their romantic hopes with each other. When Charles learned of the relationship, he was furious and set about doing everything he could to prevent the marriage from taking place. Grace had been a servant, and Charles felt that if John married someone from a lower class, it could cause the Methodist movement to split. A marriage to Grace Murray, he argued, was unthinkable for someone as important as John Wesley.

Astonishingly, in the midst of this tug-of-war for Grace's heart, John Wesley and John Bennet managed to put their personal differences aside and work side by side sharing the gospel in the face of great opposition. In October 1749, as he and John Bennet were in Bolton, John Wesley made the following entry in his journal.

We came to Bolton about five in the evening. We had no sooner entered the main street, than we perceived the lions at Rochdale were lambs in comparison to those at Bolton. Such rage and bitterness I scarce ever saw before, in any creatures that bore the form of men.

They followed us in full cry to the house where we went; and as soon as we were gone in, took possession of all the avenues to it, and filled the street from one end to the other. After some time the waves did not roar quite so loud. Mr. Perronet thought he might then venture out. They immediately closed in, threw him down, and rolled him in the mire; so that when he scrambled from them, and got into the house again, one could scarce tell what or who he was. When the first stone came among us through the window, I expected a shower to follow; and the rather, because they had now procured a bell to call their whole forces together. But they did not design to carry on the attack at a distance: Presently one ran up and told us the mob had burst into the house: He added, that they had got John Bennet in the midst of them. They had; and he laid hold on the opportunity to tell them of "the terrors of the Lord." Meantime David Taylor engaged another part of them with smoother and softer words. Believing the time was now come, I walked down into the thickest of them. They had now filled all the rooms below. I called for a chair. The winds were hushed, and all was calm and still. My heart was filled with love, my eyes with tears, and my mouth with arguments. They were amazed, they were ashamed, they were melted down, they

devoured every word. What a turn was this!
O how did God change the counsel of the old
Ahithophel into foolishness; and bring all the
drunkards, swearers, Sabbath-breakers, and
mere sinners in the place, to hear of his plenteous redemption!

Eventually it was Grace Murray who made the
decision as to whom she would marry. She chose
John Bennet, effectively breaking John Wesley's
heart. Still, John didn't rule out the possibility of
marrying one day. And in early 1751 John met Molly
Vazeille, a forty-one-year-old widow with four
grown children. John had observed her to be a pious
woman, dedicated to helping the sick. Surprisingly,
John himself was soon in need of Molly's help. After
preaching at the foundry one evening, he slipped on
a patch of ice, badly spraining his ankle. Unable to
walk, he was carried to Molly's home to convalesce.
On February 19, 1751, John and Molly were married.
John hoped that his marriage to Molly marked the
beginning of a long and useful partnership. This,
however, was not to be the case.

Chapter 14

Troubled Relationships

A Methodist preacher cannot answer to God if he preaches one sermon less or travels one day less in a married state than in a single state," John told his new wife. And he meant it. Barely a month after marrying Molly, and still limping badly from his ankle injury, John left to clarify his intentions for the Methodist movement. Some Methodist preachers were telling their followers that the Methodists would soon split with the Church of England and become their own denomination. There was nothing John wanted to avoid more.

While he was away, John wrote Molly many letters. The letters were loving, and in them he reminded his new wife to act the part of a preacher's wife. At first Molly was flattered to receive so much discipleship attention from her husband, but she soon tired of it. Being Mrs. John Wesley was much more work than she had ever imagined.

In an attempt to make their marriage stronger, in 1752 Molly agreed to accompany John on a four-month tour of northern England and the Midlands. She lasted six weeks on the trip before returning to Bristol, where her son had become ill.

Meanwhile, friction was growing between John and Charles Wesley. Charles, always the more conservative of the two, resented the level of control John tried to exert over him and other Methodist preachers. In secret Charles called his brother "Pope John," and he urged others to stand against him. Of course this led to conflict between the two brothers, and John wrote a stern letter to Charles about the issue.

> Either act really in connection with me, or never pretend it. Rather disclaim it, and openly avow you do and will not. By acting in connection with me, I mean take counsel with me once or twice a year as to the places where you will labor. Hear my advice before you fix [your destinations], whether you take it or not. At present you are so far from this that I do not even know when and where you intend to go.

The second anniversary of John and Molly's marriage passed on February 19, 1753, but by November that year, John believed that he would never see his third anniversary. He had contracted an infection in his lungs from preaching in the freezing open air. A Quaker doctor prescribed country air, rest, ass's milk, and daily riding, but even though John followed this advice, he was convinced that he was dying. So sure, in fact, was he that he wrote an epitaph for his tombstone:

> Here Lieth the Body
> of
> JOHN WESLEY
> A brand plucked from the burning
> Who died of consumption in the fifty-first
>   year of his age
> Not leaving after his debts are paid
> Ten pounds behind him.
> God be merciful to me, an unprofitable
>   servant

The entire Methodist movement was affected by John's illness, and the question was raised as to who would or should be John's successor. Charles Wesley's name was brought forward, but Charles rejected the idea outright, arguing that he did not have his older brother's physical stamina, intellect, or preaching talents. Besides, Charles had other matters pressing on his mind. His only child, eighteen-month-old Jackie, had died of smallpox, and now his wife was seriously ill with the same disease.

As it turned out, the question about leadership succession didn't need to be resolved, at least for the time being, because John did not die from the infection. He began to make a recovery, and by March 1754 he was well enough to begin preaching again, though it would be another year before he would leave southern England for places farther afield. And Sally Wesley, Charles's wife, also made a full recovery from her bout of smallpox.

In April 1755 John and Molly set out on an extensive tour of the Midlands and northern England. But Molly, who was unaccustomed to the way of life on the road, proved to be a poor choice of traveling companion for John. John wrote to a friend explaining why the difficult traveling conditions strained his and Molly's relationship.

> In my last journey north all of my patience was put to the proof, again and again.... I am content with whatever...I meet with...and this must be the spirit of all who take journeys with me. If a dinner ill-dressed, a hard bed, a poor room, a shower of rain or a dirty road, will put them out of humor, it lays a burden on me.... To have such persons at my ear, fretting and murmuring at everything, it is like tearing the flesh off my bones.

The annual conference for Methodist leaders was held that year in Leeds, and the conference proceedings revolved most around the issue of whether the Methodists should stay a part of the Church of England or sever that connection. John presented sixty-two reasons why the societies should stay within the Church of England. But even though he labeled himself a reformer within the Church of England and not the founder of a new denomination, John outlined four reasons that would serve as grounds to split off and become a separate group: Methodists should always be free to (1) preach outdoors, (2) pray without using the Book of Common Prayer, (3) form and manage their own societies, and (4) allow laymen to preach.

John acknowledged that if the Church of England authorities tried to restrict any or all of these activities, Methodists might well have to leave and form their own denomination. He made clear, however, that that time had not yet come. Charles was displeased that John would even open the door to the possibility of leaving the Church of England at some future time. As a result, he walked out of the conference in protest, declaring, "I have done with conferences forever."

John, though, was adamant that he would make the Methodist societies independent before he would allow the leaders of the Church of England to dictate to those societies what they could and could not do. He bid Charles farewell with the words, "It is probable the point will now speedily be determined concerning the Church. For if we must either *dissent* or *be silent*, it is all over. Adieu."

As he continued his travels after the conference, John found that the message of staying within the Church of England had not always made it to the rank-and-file members of the Methodist societies.

When he next visited Newcastle, he discovered that a number of the societies there had already quit the church, with the false understanding that this move had John's blessing. John tried to correct the members' wrong impression of what he thought about the matter, but he could see that it was only a matter of time before the situation would come to a head and a split from the Church of England would possibly take place. But for the time being, John reminded himself that he indeed did not want to be labeled as the founder of a new denomination but recognized as a reformer from within the existing state church.

Later in 1755 John toured Ireland once again, encouraged by the new Methodist societies springing up there and trying to win over Catholics to Methodist ways.

Charles Wesley, on the other hand, spent the year touring England, trying to undo what his brother had done in his refusal to fully and unconditionally endorse the Church of England. It was a thankless task, as he found that many members of the societies he visited were eager to separate and form their own denomination. In frustration, Charles ended his years of being an itinerant preacher and settled in Bristol to oversee the Methodist societies there and to write hymns.

While Charles was prepared to alter his priorities so that he could spend more time with his wife, John was not. His marriage to Molly had become more strained. Eventually Molly reached the point where she no longer wanted to live with John, and with money she had inherited from her first husband, she returned to an independent life. John continued his preaching and organizing.

The year 1763 found John writing what would be called the *Large Minutes,* a set of statements about Methodist beliefs and practices that would serve as the standard by which all decisions were to be made for many years to come. When the document was complete, a copy of it was given to each Methodist lay preacher as a guide for how he should conduct himself within the society.

John loaded copies of the *Large Minutes* into his saddlebags and set out once again to visit the Methodist societies throughout England. In 1764, at the age of sixty-one, he recorded in his journal the events of a typical day on the road.

I took a horse a little after four [in the morning] and about two [in the afternoon] preached in the market-place of Llanidloes [about 40] miles from Shrewsbury. At three we rode through the mountains to Fountainhead.... We mounted again about seven. [We got lost and] ended in the edge of a bog.... An honest man, instantly mounting his horse, galloped before us, up hill and down, till he brought us into a road, which he said led straight to Roes-fair. We rode on, till another met us, and said, "No, this is the way to Aberystwith.... You must turn back and ride to that yonder bridge. The master of the little house near the bridge directed us to the next village.... [Later, after nine o'clock at night,] having wandered an hour upon the mountain, through rocks, and bogs, and precipices, we...got back to the little house near the bridge. [It now] being full of drunken, roaring miners; and neither grass, nor hay nor corn.... We hired one of [the miners] to walk with us to Roes-fair, though he was miserably drunk, till falling all his length in a purling stream, he came tolerably to his senses. Between eleven and twelve we came to the inn.... [The next morning we discovered] the mule was cut in several places and my mare was bleeding like a pig, from a wound...made, it seems, by a pitchfork.

This strenuous trip was one of the many John took. In fact, at his advanced age he was still riding about three thousand miles per year, preaching over eight hundred sermons and encouraging the hundred preachers under his care. No matter the conditions, John was determined to preach the gospel to ordinary people and spur them on to live holy lives. He had come a long way from when, decades earlier, he had encountered the faith of the Moravians and had doubted his worth as a Christian. Now his worth could be counted in the lives of the many men, women, and children who, as a result of John's efforts, had faith in Jesus Christ.

The years passed, each one as busy as the last. John finally sent two itinerant Methodist preachers to the American colonies to organize the Methodist societies springing up there. Until this point he had sidestepped the issue of expanding overseas. Some Methodists had emigrated to the Caribbean islands and established societies there, as had British soldiers posted to serve in Canada and the other colonies of North America. But the pressure to officially organize these societies had mounted until, at the annual conference in August 1769, Richard Boardman and Joseph Pilmoor were sent to North America with money in hand to establish a Methodist meeting-house in New York.

At the same time, and much closer to home, John welcomed news of the establishment of the first Sunday school for children. Hannah Ball, one of his followers, started the school at High Wycombe, and along with spiritual subjects, the school taught reading, writing, and arithmetic. John thought that the school was a wonderful idea, because he believed that Christians should be able to read the Bible for themselves rather than rely on others to tell them what it said.

During the latter half of 1770, George Whitefield made his seventh preaching trip to North America. On September 29 he traveled from Portsmouth, New Hampshire, to Newburyport, Massachusetts. On the way he stopped to preach in the open air at Exeter, New Hampshire. Looking up, he prayed, "Lord Jesus, I am weary in thy work, but not of thy work. If I have not yet finished my course, let me go and speak for thee once more in the fields, seal thy truth, and come home and die."

George Whitefield died the following morning, worn out at fifty-six years of age. John was devastated when he received the news in England two weeks later. He remembered George as a seventeen-year-old at Oxford, unsure of himself but willing to obey God with all his heart. From that time on, George's life and John's had been intertwined. Certainly the two men had locked swords over the years regarding thorny issues. Despite their differences the two men had managed to retain their respect for each other.

John was honored to preach in London at three memorial services for George. He remembered George as the man who had started the "Great Awakening" across the Atlantic Ocean in America. John's text for the sermons was "Let me die the death of the righteous, and let my last end be like his!" (Numbers 23:10). John recorded in his journal his impressions of the first memorial service.

An immense multitude was gathered together from all corners of the town. I was at first afraid that a great part of the congregation would not be able to hear; but it pleased God to strengthen my voice that even those at the door heard distinctly. It was an awful season. All were still as night; most appeared to be deeply affected; and an impression was made on many which one would hope will not speedily be effaced. The time appointed for my beginning at the Tabernacle was half-hour after five, but it was quite filled at three; so I began at four. At first the noise was exceeding great; but it ceased when I began to speak; and my voice was again so strengthened that all who were within could hear, unless an accidental noise hindered here or there for a few moments. Oh that all may hear the voice of Him with whom are the issues of life and death; and who so loudly, by this unexpected stroke, calls all His children to love one another.

As John left the chapel on Tottenham Court Road where the memorial service was held, he thought about one of George's favorite sayings: "We are immortal till our work is done." Obviously George Whitefield's work was done, and John Wesley wondered how much more time God would grant him.

Chapter 15

A Tireless Worker

While most men and women of the time did not live to such an age, on June 17, 1770, John Wesley turned sixty-seven years old. On his birthday he made the following entry in his journal:

> I can hardly believe that I am this day entered into the sixty-eighth year of my age [meaning he turned sixty-seven]. How marvelous are the ways of God! How has He kept me even from a child! From ten to thirteen or fourteen, I had little but bread to eat, and not great plenty of that. I believe this was so far from hurting me, that it laid the foundation of lasting health. When I grew up, in consequence for reading Dr. Cheyne, I chose to eat

sparingly, and drink water. This was another great means of continuing my health, till…I was afterward brought to the brink of death by a fever, but it left me healthier than before.… Years after, I was in the third stage of consumption;… it pleased God to remove this also. Since that time I have known neither pain nor sickness, am now healthier than I was forty years ago. This hath God wrought!

Charles Wesley was also still alive, as were three of John's sisters, Emilia, Martha, and Anne, though the following year Emilia would die at seventy-nine years of age, severing one more of the ties to the days of living in the rectory at Epworth.

Despite his age, John continued on determinedly, gathering and preparing anything he had ever written to be published in a collective work. When it was finally done, the *Collective Works* filled thirty-two volumes. Over the years John had earned a handsome sum of money from his writing—up to fourteen hundred pounds a year. Yet even with this money, he had stayed true to his ideals of simple living. He kept thirty pounds for himself to live on, the same amount he had set for himself back in college, and gave the rest of it away to Methodist charities. When questioned as to why he did not keep a little more of the money for personal "comforts," John always gave the same reply: "Money never stays with me, it would burn me if it did. I throw it out of my hands as soon as possible, lest it find a way into my heart."

While he labored away in England, John kept a watchful eye on what was happening in the American colonies. In March 1770, five colonists had been killed when British troops opened fire on them in what came to be known as the Boston Massacre. As the possibility of a full-scale rebellion loomed in America, many people in the colonies turned to the Methodist societies for strength and stability. In response to this increase in the numbers of people joining the societies, John sent two more preachers to America from England. They were twenty-six-year-old Francis Asbury and twenty-four-year-old Thomas Coke. The two men were from very different backgrounds. Thomas was a graduate of Jesus College, Oxford, and an ordained clergyman in the Church of England, while Francis came from a lower-class family in Wednesbury, the site of some of the worst anti-Methodist rioting. Once they arrived in the colonies, Thomas and Francis took over running the Methodist societies in New York and Philadelphia, freeing Richard Boardman and Joseph Pilmoor to branch out to the colonies to the north and south.

Meanwhile, things were also changing in England. Methodist women were taking on a greater role in the societies. It was yet another practice that put the Methodists further at odds with the Church of England. John tried to soothe the situation by encouraging the women to use their preaching gifts while not actually crossing the line far enough to be accused of preaching, much like his mother had done back in Epworth fifty-eight years before. This was not an easy thing to do, and John wrote to one Methodist "preacher," Sarah Crosby, outlining the way that she should proceed when groups of up to two hundred people begged her to preach to them.

> When you meet again, tell them simply, "You lay me under a great difficulty. The Methodists do not allow of women preachers; neither do I take upon me any such character. But I will just nakedly tell you what is on my heart."… I do not see that you have broken any law. Go on calmly and steadily.

The crowds who thronged to hear John preach continued to grow, and in August 1773, John preached to a gathering of 32,000 people, his largest single audience ever. "Perhaps the first time that a man of seventy had been heard by thirty thousand persons at once," he noted of the occasion in his journal.

Following the Boston Massacre, tensions between the colonists in North America and the British settled down, but they began to grow again in 1773, when the British parliament passed an act that gave the East India Company a monopoly on selling tea in the colony. The act threatened the livelihood of many local tea merchants, and East India Company ships were prevented from docking and unloading their cargoes in New York and Philadelphia. In Boston a group of local citizens took matters into their own hands. On December 16, 1773, the group, disguised as Indians, boarded three East India Company ships and tossed hundreds of crates of tea into the harbor in an act that became known as the Boston Tea Party.

For the first time, open conflict between England and her American colonies began to loom on the horizon. In response to this threat, many American Methodists made their way north to Canada in the hope of avoiding war in the lower colonies.

In April 1775, fighting between the British and the colonies finally broke out in Concord and Lexington, Massachusetts. At the start of the war, John found himself surprisingly sympathetic to the rebel cause. He even wrote a letter to the secretary of state for the colonies, Lord Dartmouth, in which he said,

And whether my writing do any good or no, it need do no harm. For it rests within your Lordship's breast whether any eye but your own shall see it.

All my prejudices are against the Americans. For I am an High Churchman, the son of an High Churchman, bred up from my childhood in the highest notions of passive obedience and non-resistance. And yet, in spite of all my rooted prejudice, I cannot avoid thinking (if I think at all) that an oppressed people asked for nothing more than their legal rights, and that in the most modest and inoffensive manner which the nature of the thing would allow.

But waiving this, waiving all considerations of right and wrong, I ask, Is it common sense to use force toward the Americans?

A letter now before me says, "Four hundred of the Regulars and forty of the Militia were killed in the last skirmish." What a disproportion! And this is the first essay of raw men against regular troops!

You see, my Lord, whatever has been affirmed, these men will not be frightened. And it seems they will not be conquered so easily as was at first imagined. They will probably dispute every inch of ground, and, if they die, die sword in hand.

Indeed, some of our valiant officers say, "Two thousand men will clear America of these rebels." No, nor twenty thousand, nor perhaps treble [three times] that number, be they rebels or not. They are as strong men as you; they are as valiant as you, if not abundantly more valiant. For they are one and all enthusiasts—enthusiasts for liberty. They are calm, deliberate enthusiasts. And we know how this principle breathed into softest souls stem love of war, and thirst of vengeance, and contempt of death. We know men animated with this will leap into a fire or rush upon a cannon's mouth.

"But they have no experience of war." And how much more have our troops? How few of them ever saw a battle! "But they have no discipline." That is an entire mistake. Already they have near as much as our army. And they will learn more of it every day. So that in a short time they will understand it as well as their assailants.

However, after many meetings with his friend, the writer Samuel Johnson, John changed his mind about the war in the colonies and became a defender of British policies in North America. He even took one of Johnson's pamphlets titled *Taxation No Tyranny* and republished it under his own name with the title *A Calm Address to the American Colonies.* The pamphlet declared that the American colonists had no right to clamber for their own liberty when they held slaves in bondage.

Publication of the pamphlet caused a public outcry, not because of what the document said but because John had copied and published it without permission. In response to the criticism, John published another edition of the pamphlet, acknowledging that his friend Samuel Johnson had originally written it. The public outcry quickly died down.

John Wesley's prediction to Lord Dartmouth that the American colonists would "probably dispute every inch of ground, and, if they die, die sword in hand," however, proved accurate. In July 1776 the colonists declared their independence from Britain, and although things were not going well for them in the fight with the British, the colonists were proving to be tenacious and unpredictable fighters.

As the war in the American colonies raged on, John urged the Methodist leaders there not to take sides. But he made this all but impossible for them by continuing to print his anti-American pamphlets and then having the pamphlets distributed in the colonies.

Despite John's anti-American stance, the number of people joining the Methodist societies in the colonies continued to grow, from 955 in 1775 to 4,379 in 1777. This was because the Methodists in America did not feel the same allegiance to the Church of England and as a result acted more or less as an independent church. Indeed, the status of Methodists in North America was a matter that John Wesley could not ignore indefinitely, though at the time other matters at home were proving more pressing.

One of these matters, which took up a lot of John's time, was the building of a new Methodist chapel in London. By 1776, it was obvious to all that the foundry chapel was old and dilapidated and in need of replacing. John made an appeal to the Methodist societies throughout England to give money toward the building of a new chapel to serve as the head-quarters of Methodism. The money began to roll in, and on April 21, 1777, in driving rain, John laid the foundation stone for the new structure, which was to be called Wesley's Chapel. The new chapel was situated on an acre of land on Royal Row (City Road), where windmills had previously stood, and about fifty yards north of the foundry. Throughout the following months, John oversaw the construction of the new chapel until its official opening on November 1, 1778. The building was a large, plain chapel that could seat two thousand people. And next door to the chapel was a house for John to live in.

At the same time as Wesley's Chapel was going up, another project occupied John—the publishing of a Methodist magazine that he named the *Arminian Magazine*. The publication was designed to advance Methodist ideas and refute Calvinist thinking. John wrote many of the articles in the magazine himself. One of the first articles he penned was about Old Jeffrey, the ghost who had haunted the Epworth rectory in his youth.

Two years later, in 1780, John published *A Collection of Hymns for the Use of the People Called Methodists*. The hymnal was a collection of 525 hymns: seven of them were written by Isaac Watts, one was by John's brother Samuel, one was by his father, nineteen were German hymns John had translated, sixteen John had written himself, and the remainder were the works of his brother Charles. It was a great day for the brothers to see so many of their words in print, since they both believed that hymns had the power to implant themselves into the hearts of even the most illiterate hearers. Most of the hymns in the new hymnal had been published in some form before, but John, in his usual practical way, introduced the hymnal as "not so large as to be either cumbersome, or expensive: and…large enough to contain such a weight of hymns as will not soon be worn threadbare."

A year later, in October 1781, John returned to London from a preaching trip to Bristol to learn of his wife's death. The couple had lived apart for many years, and John was saddened by her passing.

By now John was an old man and anticipated his own death at any time, especially since he had already lived longer than either of his parents. But on his seventy-ninth birthday he was still going strong, and he noted in his journal,

> I entered into my eightieth year [that is, turned seventy-nine], but, blessed be God, my time is not labor and sorrow. I find no more pain nor bodily infirmities than at five-and-twenty. This I still impute (1) to the power of God, fitting me for what he calls me to; (2) to my still traveling four or five thousand miles a year; (3) to my sleeping, night or day, whenever I want it; (4) to my rising at a set hour; and (5) to my constant preaching, particularly in the morning....

Then John added,

> Lastly, evenness of temper. I feel and grieve, but, by the grace of God, I fret at nothing. But still, "the help that is done upon earth he doeth it himself." And this he doeth in answer to many prayers.

A fellow preacher, John Hampson, wrote a description of the aged John Wesley. He depicted

John as a surprisingly strong, muscular man for his age with "a narrow, plaited stock, a coat with a small upright collar, no buckles at the knees, no silk or velvet in any part of his apparel, and a head as white as snow, gave the idea of something primitive and apostolical; while an air of neatness and cleanliness was diffused over his whole person."

Even after his eightieth birthday, John did not stop his relentless preaching schedule. He did allow his friends to buy him a carriage, but more often than not he commandeered one of the horses pulling the carriage and rode on ahead. Nothing was more invigorating to him than a good horse ride of fifty miles or more.

As John toured England, Ireland, and Wales, the American colonies were never far from his mind. With help from the French, the American rebels in the colonies won their struggle for freedom, and Britain had begrudgingly recognized their independence. This outcome surprised John, who had come to believe that Britain was fighting for a just cause. However, he decided to focus on the future and what would happen to the Methodists in America, who were still officially part of the Church of England. Questions about the issue swirled in John's mind. Should the Methodists in America still be bound by the laws of the English Church and subject to the rule of King George III, who was not only the English monarch but also the head of the Church of England? John knew that he was not the only one grappling with such questions and that answers would have to be found soon.

Chapter 16

Active Till the End

The 1780s finally brought an end to the persecution of Methodists by angry mobs. Now, wherever John went he was honored. During his final trip to Ireland the mayors of Dublin and Cork accorded John civic honors, and everywhere he went, John was a coveted guest. From Dublin John made a nine-week tour through sixty towns and villages, preaching a hundred sermons, six of them in the open air, and once in a place that he said was "large but not elegant, a cow house."

Seventeen eighty-four was the year that John finally faced the fact that he would have to make plans for Methodism to survive after his death. He decided to write *A Deed of Declaration*, which he executed on February 28, 1784. The deed legally defined the "Conference of the people called Methodists" and declared "how the succession and identity thereof is to be continued." The document listed the names of a hundred preachers who were to oversee the societies and trust property after his death. John had been carefully training up these preachers for this responsibility, and he continued to do so.

Four months later, in July, John was particularly touched when he visited Robert Raikes's Sunday school. Raikes was a crusading editor of the *Gloucester Journal* who had become frustrated reporting on criminal activity and was convinced that much of what he reported on was the result of poverty and a lack of education. In response he started Sunday schools, much as Hannah Ball had done fifteen years before, to teach child factory workers how to read and write. Many of the children's parents joined the children at the Sunday lessons. John recorded in his journal his thoughts on what he had seen.

> I stepped into the Sunday school, which contains two hundred and forty children, taught every Sunday by several masters, and superintended by the curate. So, many children in one parish are restrained from open sin, and taught a little good manners at least, as well as to read the Bible. I find these schools springing up wherever I go. Perhaps God may have a deeper end therein than men are aware of. Who knows but some of these schools may become nurseries for Christians?

When asked what he found so touching about the Sunday school, John replied, "I reverence the young because they may be useful after I am dead. Take care of the rising generation."

Thomas Coke, whom John had dispatched to North America to help organize the Methodist societies, returned to England. On September 1, 1784, a momentous step was taken at Bristol regarding the Methodists in the newly independent United States. At Mr. Castleman's home on Dighton Street in Bristol, John laid his hands on Thomas and ordained him superintendent for the "Church of God under our care in North America." Furthermore, John commissioned Thomas to return to North America and ordain Francis Asbury as his joint superintendent, though he cautioned that neither man should use the title *bishop*.

When he returned to the United States from England, Thomas carried with him a letter from John Wesley to the American Methodists which read in part, "As our American brethren are now totally disentangled both from the State and from the English hierarchy, we dare not entangle them again either with the one or the other. They are now at full liberty simply to follow the Scriptures and primitive Church; and we judge it best that they should stand fast in that liberty wherewith God has so strangely made them free."

John continued his efforts to make the American Methodists free from any connection to the Church of England by rewriting the Book of Common Prayer, calling it *The Sunday Service of the Methodists in North America*. The new version was shorter and replaced the terms *priest* and *bishop* with *superintendent* and *elder*. It also omitted fifteen of the thirty-nine articles of faith, along with the list of holy days that were celebrated on the church calendar.

Meanwhile things were moving quickly in North America. Although John had not thought it necessary, the American Methodists decided to vote on the ordination of Francis Asbury and Thomas Coke before accepting it. The vote was unanimous, but the action sent a clear message back to England that while American Methodists would be loyal to John Wesley as their founder, they intended to live in "connection" with him, not in subordination to him.

The following year, at the Christmas conference of 1786, the Methodist leaders in the United States decided to found a school to educate the sons of Methodist preachers and orphans, much like the boarding school John had established at Kingswood. They named the new institution Cokesbury College—a blending of Coke's and Asbury's names.

The following year John took a step that hastened the official break between Methodists and the Church of England. In an attempt to safeguard his chapels and preachers, John secured licenses for them as Dissenter meetinghouses. This meant that Methodism was no longer an extension of the Church of England but was a Dissenter denomination. John took this step to stop Methodist meetinghouses from being taken over by the Church of England upon his death.

Just as he had been with the ordination of Francis Asbury and Thomas Coke, Charles Wesley was displeased that his brother had decided to break away from the mother church. The decision led to a rift between the two "giants of Methodism," one that unfortunately was not healed before Charles died in March 1788. John was traveling in the north of England at the time and did not hear the news of Charles's death in time to get back for the funeral. Instead of being held in the newly licensed Methodist City Road Chapel (Wesley's Chapel), Charles Wesley's funeral service was held at St. Marylebone's in London, an Anglican church. And eight Anglican ministers carried Charles's coffin into the churchyard, where Charles was buried in consecrated ground.

Charles Wesley left behind a legacy of 6,500 hymns, many of which John published for him. Three of his most popular hymns were "Hark! The Herald Angels Sing," "Jesus, Lover of My Soul," and "O for a Thousand Tongues to Sing."

Knowing that Charles understood the importance and urgency of preaching, John continued with his tour of northern England, arriving in Bolton three weeks after the funeral. There, as a children's choir prepared to sing one of Charles's hymns, John stood and read the first verse:

Come, O Thou Traveler unknown,
Whom still I hold, but cannot see:
My company before is gone,
And I am left alone with Thee.

John struggled to read on, but his brother's words affected him deeply. Quietly he laid aside the hymnal, sat down, put his head in his hands, and wept openly for Charles.

On January 1, 1790, John wrote in his journal, "I am now an old man, decayed from head to foot. My eyes are dim; my right hand shakes much; my mouth is hot and dry every morning; I have a lingering fever almost every day; my motion is weak and slow. However, blessed be God, I do not slack my labor; I can preach and write still."

John continued to rise at four each morning, and he traveled to Scotland and back before his eighty-seventh birthday on June 17, 1790. By then, however, he thought that his strength "probably will not return in this world. But I feel no pain from head to foot; only it seems nature is exhausted, and, humanly speaking, will sink more and more till the weary springs of life stand still."

John also made another visit to Epworth, though it was with mixed emotions. The rectory at Epworth no longer rang with the sounds of his lively and talented family; only he and his sister Martha remained alive. Still, there were highlights on the trip. The local Methodists escorted him on foot around the fens from village to village, singing as they went. John preached in the village squares and greeted friends and admirers everywhere he went with the verse, "Little children, love one another."

Later in 1790 John attended the annual Methodist conference in Bristol. At the gathering, the latest statistics on Methodist membership were read into the official record. In England there were now 71,463 Methodist members; in the United States, 43,260; and in other parts of the world, including Scotland, the Caribbean, and Canada, 5,350. When the business of the conference was over, John, who for the past forty-six years had directed its deliberations, penned his signature to the conference minutes. His hand was wobbly now, but his vision to increase the number of Methodists was as sure as ever.

During the remainder of the year, John traveled and preached in Wales, the Midlands, Lincolnshire, Scotland, and the Isle of Wight. On October 6, 1790, at midday he preached at an open-air service held under an ash tree in the churchyard at Winchelsea, Sussex, so that people at work could hear him as they ate their lunch. The text he chose for his sermon was "The kingdom of heaven is at hand; repent ye, and believe the gospel."

By 1791, John was confined to London, preaching inside chapels where he was less likely to catch a chill. In his old age, John was still concerned with the state of the Methodist movement, greatly desiring unity among its members. He expressed this in a letter to America dated February 1, in which he wrote, "Lose no opportunity of declaring to all men that the Methodists are one people in all the world, and that it is their full determination so to continue, though mountains rise, and oceans roll, to sever us in vain."

Although his traveling days were over, John continued to take a lively interest in the world around him. Early in the new year he read the autobiography of an African slave named Gustavas Vassa. John had helped pay the publishing costs for the book, and it gave him great pleasure to finally read it.

In response to what he read in the book, John dictated a letter to William Wilberforce, a Methodist convert and member of Parliament who was championing the cause of opposing England's participation in slavery anywhere in the world.

February 24, 1791

MY DEAR SIR: Unless the divine Power has raised you up to be as Athanasius, *contra roundurn*, I see not how you can go through your glorious enterprise in opposing that execrable villainy, which is the scandal of religion, of England, and of human nature. Unless God has raised you up for this very thing, you will be worn out by the opposition of men and devils; but if God be for you, who can be against you? Are all of them together stronger than God? O "be not weary in well-doing." Go on, in the name of God, and in the power of his might, till even American slavery, the vilest that ever saw the sun, shall vanish away before it.

Reading this morning a tract, wrote by a poor African, I was particularly struck by that circumstance—that a man who has a black skin, being wronged or outraged by a white man, can have no redress, it being a law in our colonies that the oath of a black against a white goes for nothing. What villainy is this!

That He who has guided you from your youth up may continue to strengthen you in this and all things, is the prayer of, dear sir, your affectionate servant, JOHN WESLEY.

The late winter of 1791 was severe, and John was often ill with coughs and colds. Each bout of sickness seemed to weaken him a little more, and John sensed that the end was near for him. On the morning of March 1, he called for a pen and ink, but he was not strong enough to write. A Methodist leader, Betsy Ritchie, asked what he wanted to write. With his only surviving sister, Martha, and Charles's widow, Sally, at his side, John gathered his remaining strength and cried out, "The best of all is, God is with us."

When Sally moistened his lips, he repeated the thanksgiving that he had always recited after a meal. "We thank thee, O Lord, for these and all thy mercies; bless the Church and the king; and grant us truth and peace, through Jesus Christ our Lord, forever and ever."

John made it through the night, and on the morning of Wednesday, March 2, 1791, the leading members of the Methodist Church gathered at his bedside. John lifted his arms and imparted a blessing to them. "Lift up your heads, O ye gates; and be ye lift up, ye everlasting doors; and this heir of glory shall come in!" The words said, at eighty-seven years of age, John Wesley took his last breath. It was an appropriate passing for a Methodist—no complaining, no admission of pain, just joyous anticipation of entering his Savior's eternal presence.

John's funeral was planned for Wednesday, March 9, and the day before the service, John's body was laid in honor in City Road Chapel. Ten thousand mourners passed by his coffin, eager for one last look at their leader.

The organizers of the funeral realized that the chapel would be overrun with mourners and secretly scheduled the service for five o'clock in the morning. The Reverend John Richardson, one of the clergymen who had helped John for nearly thirty years, officiated at the service. When he came to the ceremonial words, "Forasmuch as it hath pleased Almighty God to take unto himself the soul of our dear brother," with profound feeling he substituted the word *father* for *brother*, and as he did so, the gathered throng began to sob.

John Wesley, the spiritual father of so many, was still at last. During his lifetime he had ridden a quarter of a million miles on horseback, stopping along the way to preach over forty thousand sermons. He offered a simple form of Christianity to millions of people who were outside the influence of the churches of the day, and he had governed a movement focused on God's love and holy living that was soon to spread around the globe.

True to form, John had left meticulous directions on how his estate was to be divided. He left the bulk of his money to the Methodist general fund; forty pounds to his remaining sibling, Martha; and twenty shillings to each of "six poor men" who were to be chosen to carry his coffin. Although he asked that there be no show of mourning, the funeral organizers ignored this request and draped the City Road Chapel in black fabric. When the funeral was over, the fabric was cut up and given to sixty poor women to make themselves dresses. That, at least, John would have approved of.

At the first Methodist conference following John's death, a letter detailing John's instructions for the ongoing work of the Methodists was read aloud. In the letter, dated 1785, John warned those who would now assume positions of authority not to use their newfound power to lord it over other Methodist preachers. His final words urged them to carry on uprightly:

> I know no other way to prevent any such inconvenience than to leave these, my last words, with you. I beseech you, by the mercies of God, that you never avail yourselves of the Deed of Declaration to assume any superiority over your brethren, but let all things go on among those itinerants who choose to remain together exactly in the same manner as when I was with you, so far as circumstances will permit. In particular, I beseech you, if you ever loved me, and if you now love God and your brethren, to have no respect for persons in stationing the preachers,

in choosing children for the Kingswood
School, in disposing of the yearly contribu-
tion and the preachers' fund, or any other
public money. But do all things with a single
eye, as I have done from the beginning. Go
on thus, doing all things without prejudice or
partiality, and God will be with you even to
the end.

Ethridge, Willie (Snow). *Strange Fire: The True Story of John Wesley's Love Affair in Georgia.* New York: Vanguard Press, 1971.

Harmon, Rebecca Lamar. *Susanna, Mother of the Wesleys.* Nashville: Abingdon Press, 1968.

Hattersley, Roy. *The Life of John Wesley: A Brand from the Burning.* New York: Doubleday, 2003.

McReynolds, Kathy. *Susanna Wesley.* Bloomington, Minn.: Bethany House Publishers, 1998.

Miller, Basil. *John Wesley: The World His Parish.* Grand Rapids: Zondervan, 1943.

Tomkins, Stephen. *John Wesley: A Biography.* Grand Rapids: William B. Eerdmans, 2003.

Wellman, Sam. *John Wesley: Founder of the Methodist Church.* Uhrichsville, Ohio: Barbour Publishing, 1997.

Wesley, John. Edited by Elisabeth Jay. *The Journal of John Wesley: A Selection.* New York: Oxford University Press, 1987.

About the Authors

Janet and Geoff Benge are a husband-and-wife writing team with more than twenty years of writing experience. Janet is a former elementary-school teacher. Geoff holds a degree in history. Originally from New Zealand, the Benges spent ten years serving with Youth With A Mission. They have two daughters, Laura and Shannon, and an adopted son, Lito. They make their home in the Orlando, Florida, area.